SPEECH

COMMUNICATION

MADE SIMPLE

1

PAULETTE DALE, PH.D., PROFESSOR EMERITUS

MIAMI DADE COLLEGE

Speech Communication Made Simple 1

Pearson Education, 10 Bank Street, White Plains, NY 10606

Staff credits: The people who made up the *Speech Communication Made Simple* team—representing editorial, production, design, marketing, and manufacturing services—are Tracey Cataldo, Dave Dickey, Nancy Flaggman, Amy McCormick, Lise Minovitz, Liza Pleva, and Jane Townsend.

Development: Lida Baker
Cover design: Mary Ann Smith
Text composition: S4Carlisle Publishing Services
Illustrations: Roger Penwill
Text font: 11/13 pt Minion Pro
Cover Photos: (top) Ljupco Smokovski/Shutterstock, (center) Tatiana Popova/Shutterstock, (bottom) Winston Link/Shutterstock.
Photo Credits: Page 12 (top) Mark R. Williamson/Alamy, (bottom) cenker atila/Shutterstock; p. 13 Makarova Viktoria (Vikarus)/Shutterstock; p. 18 (left) Yuri Arcurs/Shutterstock, (center) Yuri Arcurs/Shutterstock, (right) YUYI/Shutterstock; p. 19 Courtesy of Marie Knepper; p. 28 kovaleff/Fotolia; p. 29 (top) charobnica/Shutterstock, (top center) WilleeCole/Shutterstock, (bottom) .shock/Shutterstock; p. 31 Margo Harrison/Shutterstock; p. 32 Peter Hermes Furian/Fotolia; p. 70 Lisa F. Young/Shutterstock; p. 101 Karlowac/Shutterstock; p. 102 (top) Zurijeta/Shutterstock, (top center) Jack.Q/Shutterstock, (bottom center) Phase4Photography/Shutterstock, (bottom) Nadezhda V. Kulagina/Shutterstock; p. 115 SuperStock/Glow Images.

Library of Congress Cataloging-in-Publication Data

Dale, Paulette.
    Speech communication made simple. 1 / Paulette Dale.—1st ed.
        p. cm.
    ISBN: 0-13-286168-2
    ISBN: 0-13-286169-0
        1. Public speaking—Problems, exercises, etc.   2. Oral communication—Problems, exercises, etc.
    3. English language—Textbooks for foreign speakers.   I. Title.

    PN4121.D327 2012
    302.2'242—dc23

                                                                                    2012024143

ISBN 10:   0-13-286168-2
ISBN 13: 978-0-13-286168-7

Printed in the United States of America
2 3 4 5 6 7 8 9 10—V011—18 17 16 15 14

PEARSON ELT ON THE WEB

PearsonELT.com offers a wide range of classroom resources and professional development materials. Access course-specific websites, product information, and Pearson offices around the world.

Visit us at **www.pearsonELT.com**.

CONTENTS

PREFACE: TO THE TEACHER

Speech Communication Made Simple 1 is a practical, user-friendly presentation-skills course for intermediate ESL students. It features rich academic content, varied activities, and a step-by-step approach to building students' confidence as speakers.

Chapter Organization

Each chapter contains sections designed to help students improve their speech communication abilities and express themselves effectively in front of others. Exercises and assignments prepare students for the ultimate chapter goal: the preparation and delivery of a presentation to the class.

The **Chapter Challenge** serves as an introduction to the chapter topic. It provides an overview of the objectives of the chapter.

The **Presentation Preview** provides an engaging introduction to the speech assignment. It helps students consider the topic of the presentation and relate it to their own experiences. It includes a sample presentation (a speech, interview, or discussion) that follows the organization and contains the content required in the chapter assignment.

The **Pronunciation Practice** section offers instruction and practice in a selected American-English pronunciation pattern. The pronunciation points selected are those that are difficult for most non-native speakers of English. Students are encouraged to practice the pronunciation skills presented in each chapter when preparing and delivering their speeches.

The **Playing with Sayings** section presents idiomatic sayings in popular use. The related activities help students understand the sayings and use them to enhance their spoken communication. Students are encouraged to use one or more of these sayings in their presentations.

The **Presentation Project** provides specific guidelines and useful language for students to follow in order to prepare, practice, and deliver their own presentations on the assigned topic. Step-by-step instructions are given for choosing and researching a topic, citing sources, using transitions, and outlining information. Instructions vary by chapter and directly relate to the nature and complexity of the assignment.

Book Contents

The chapters included in *Speech Communication Made Simple 1* are as follows:

Chapter 1: Getting Started is designed to help students overcome stage fright and succeed at public speaking.

Chapter 2: Effective Speech Delivery has numerous activities to help students improve their use of eye contact, posture, gestures, and voice so that they speak more effectively.

Chapter 3: Don't Just Tell Me, Show Me! gives general guidelines for the effective use of speech aids (both audio and visual) to enhance presentations.

Chapter 4: Interesting Interviews teaches students to identify different types of questions used by interviewers, conduct an interview, and prepare a speech about the information learned in the interview.

Chapter 5: Explain It! gives step-by-step procedures for identifying a problem, analyzing its causes, suggesting solutions, and preparing a speech that presents information in a comprehensible and memorable way.

Chapter 6: Demonstrate It! presents guidelines for identifying a process or skill and preparing and organizing a "how to" speech.

Chapter 7: Communicating Across Cultures helps students understand and appreciate the diverse beliefs and customs of people from different backgrounds in order to communicate across cultures more effectively.

Chapter 8: Convince Me! gives step-by-step procedures for preparing a speech that persuades others to change a belief or a behavior using Monroe's Motivated Sequence.

Chapter 9: Let's Discuss It! provides students with practice in the process of brainstorming to produce ideas. The chapter also teaches students how to research a topic and how to lead and participate in an organized group discussion about it.

Chapter 10: Tell Me a Story teaches the basics of effective story telling, including plot development from start to finish and effective use of voice, gestures, and facial expressions to make a story come alive.

Approach

Speech Communication Made Simple 1 incorporates a scaffolded approach to the development of students' public speaking skills. At the beginning of each chapter, students participate in a directed discussion of a model presentation as a prelude to preparing, writing, and delivering their own speeches. The next series of steps focus on skill building. Students read guidelines for selecting an appropriate topic; learn language needed to speak about the topic; fill out worksheets to help them organize information into an introduction, body, and conclusion; and prepare note cards for use during their speech. In the practice phase of the lesson, students practice their presentation out loud and complete a speech checklist to confirm all required presentation elements are included. Having worked through all these steps, students are ready to deliver their speech.

Components

In addition to its interactive activities and extensive speaking assignments, *Speech Communication Made Simple 1* offers an array of components to facilitate ease of teaching and learning. These components include:

- Evaluation forms in the Appendix providing suggested evaluation criteria for each presentation
- A DVD in the back of the book with MP3 audio for all the sample speeches, pronunciation, and listening activities
- An online *Teacher's Manual* that includes chapter-by-chapter teaching suggestions, quizzes, answer keys, and the audioscripts for the listening exercises in the student book.

INTRODUCTION: TO THE STUDENT

At some point in your life, you will probably have to make a speech in front of an audience. You might want to convince people to change their opinion about a topic or demonstrate how to make or do something. You might need to teach an audience new information about a subject or share a personal experience with them. Maybe you will be asked to participate in a group discussion at school, work, a place of worship, or a club. In any of these cases, you will need to be able to organize your thoughts and express them so that others can easily understand and remember them. As you can see, the ability to make a presentation before an audience is an important skill to have in life.

If the ability to make a presentation is important in your life, then *Speech Communication Made Simple 1* is for you! Among many other skills, this book teaches you how to:

- choose a topic that will interest your listeners and decide what to say about it;
- organize your thoughts and information so that listeners can follow your ideas easily;
- get your audience's attention, develop the body of your presentation, and conclude your speech in a memorable way;
- use your voice, natural gestures, good posture, and eye contact to "wow" your audience.

Most important of all, *Speech Communication Made Simple 1* will help you overcome your fears about speaking before a group and give you the self-confidence to take advantage of opportunities to speak in public.

The more effort you put into studying and practicing the skills *Speech Communication Made Simple 1* teaches you, the more you will benefit. Although you might be nervous about the idea of standing before an audience and making a speech, your fears will fade as you progress through this book. By the time you have finished, you will be very proud of yourself and of your progress.

As you work through this book you will have many chances to speak in class. The assignments will give you confidence and help you to improve future speeches. With the help of this book and your teacher, you will learn how to select topics, make them interesting to your audience, get over problem spots, and improve your ability to speak in front of a group—large or small. I hope you enjoy all the fun activities in *Speech Communication Made Simple 1*.

Let's begin!

SCOPE AND SEQUENCE

Chapter	Title	Speech Genre	Pronunciation Practice	
1	GETTING STARTED	Autobiography	[i] and [I]	
2	EFFECTIVE SPEECH DELIVERY	Meaningful Object	Final Consonant Sounds	
3	DON'T JUST TELL ME, SHOW ME!	My Worst Fear	Regular Past-Tense Verbs	
4	INTERESTING INTERVIEWS	Speech About an Interview	Intonation in Questions	
5	EXPLAIN IT!	Informative	Compound Nouns	
6	DEMONSTRATE IT!	Informative (How to)	Voiced and voiceless *th*	
7	COMMUNICATING ACROSS CULTURES	Culture Conflict	[u] and [ʊ]	
8	CONVINCE ME!	Persuasive	[b], [v], and [w]	
9	LET'S DISCUSS IT!	Group Discussion	Final -*s* as [s], [z] and [əz]	
10	TELL ME A STORY	A Fable	[h]	

Playing with Sayings	Useful Language
as easy as pie, like sardines, foot the bill, stand on one's own two feet, seeing is believing	Conversation Starters; Beginning Your Speech; Concluding Your Speech; Introducing Your Photos
in over one's head, lose one's head, out of hand, lend a hand, one's heart isn't in it	Getting Listeners' Attention
saved the day, crossed one's fingers, counted one's blessings, melted in one's mouth, lifted one's spirits	Concluding Your Speech
Where's the fire? Do you read me? What comes to mind? What's new? What's up?	Introducing Restatements
have butterflies in one's stomach, like a deer in headlights, in a heartbeat, one's worst nightmare, hit a roadblock	Preview Statements Summary Statements
the life of the party, to throw in the towel, to put two and two together, through thick and thin, to be under the weather	Stating Your Topic; Previewing the Body of the Speech; Signaling the Steps; Emphasizing Difficult Steps
too good to be true, pull the wool over one's eyes, put one's foot in one's mouth, get to the point, pull some strings	Beginning the Body of the Speech
with bells on, wear out one's welcome, white lie, out of the blue, in black and white	Attention Getters
go to pieces, on the books, make tracks, pull some strings, all ears	Providing Feedback and Reinforcement; Adding Information; Group Leader Transitions
hold your horses, hang in there, to hold one's tongue, hit the nail on the head, to have high hopes	Beginning a Story

ABOUT THE AUTHOR

Paulette Dale, Ph.D, Professor Emeritus and Endowed Teaching Chair at Miami Dade College, has taught speech communication, public speaking, and pronunciation classes for international students for more than thirty-five years. She has authored a variety of textbooks and series for Pearson Education including *English Pronunciation Made Simple* and *Speech Communication Made Simple*. She has been the featured speaker at international conferences including MexTESOL, BrazTESOL, VenTESOL, PanamaTESOL, ELT Horizons in Peru, ABLA in Guatemala, and SHARE in Argentina. Dr. Dale is currently an English Language Specialist for the U.S. State Department and travels around the world conducting workshops for English language teachers. Her areas of expertise include English pronunciation, speaking, listening, and teaching young learners.

Acknowledgments

The author wishes to express her sincere gratitude and indebtedness to the many people who assisted in developing this book:

Professors Marie Knepper and James Wolf of Miami Dade College, Academic Directors Leo Mercado and Anthony Acevedo of the Instituto Cultural Peruano Norteamericano, and other colleagues who recommended valuable improvements;

My editors, Amy McCormick, Lise Minovitz, and Lida Baker, who were extremely helpful, understanding, and patient, and who helped transform the manuscript into this wonderful new book;

The following reviewers, who read the material and provided valuable feedback and suggestions for improvement: Brigitte Barshay, English Language Institute UCSD, La Jolla, California; Christina Hankwitz, St. Norbert College, De Pere, Wisconsin; Lisa Kovacs-Morgan, English Language Institute UCSD, La Jolla, California; Alice Lee, Richland College, Dallas, Texas; Sarah Saxer, Howard Community College, Columbia, Maryland; and Floria Volynskaya, Howard Community College, Columbia, Maryland;

My students, for encouraging me and for giving me many practical suggestions to help me better meet their needs;

And, finally, my family and friends for their support and encouragement throughout the project.

CHAPTER 1

GETTING STARTED

Welcome to the first day of your speech communication class! Perhaps you are feeling a bit scared about speaking in front of an audience. Don't worry! By using this book, you will soon develop the skills you need to speak effectively in front of a group. Your teacher is here to help you succeed in this class, and your classmates will soon become new friends.

CHAPTER CHALLENGE Your challenge in this chapter is to begin to develop self-confidence when speaking in public. This chapter has many suggestions to help you. By the time you complete this chapter, you will:

- learn the meaning of "stage fright"
- understand that stage fright is a normal and natural feeling
- be able to plan, prepare, and present a speech of self-introduction

I. Stage Fright

The fear of speaking in public is called *stage fright*. It is like the fear that actors feel before they go on stage. When you have to speak in front of a group, does your heart start racing? Do your hands sweat? Is your mouth dry? If so, you are not alone! Most people experience these signs of stage fright when they speak before a group. The following activities will help you overcome your fear.

ACTIVITY 1 Talk about Stage Fright

1 Discuss these questions with a partner:

   a. Have you ever had stage fright? What was the situation? What signs did you experience?

   b. What do you think causes us to have stage fright? Write three reasons below.

      1. _____

      2. _____

      3. _____

   c. What are some ways of controlling stage fright?

      1. _____

      2. _____

      3. _____

2 Share your answers with the class.

ACTIVITY 2 Mix and Mingle!

A great way to become more confident is to meet the other members of your class in a relaxed situation. In this activity you will imagine you are at a party, where you will "mix and mingle" with your classmates.

1 Set the room up for a party. You may want to bring beverages or snacks.

2 Walk around and meet your classmates. You can use the Conversation Starters in the Useful Language box to start conversations.

> **USEFUL LANGUAGE: CONVERSATION STARTERS**
>
> Hi, my name is _____. What's your name?
>
> Hello again. Can I ask you a question?
>
> Excuse me, aren't you in my (math) class?
>
> I've seen you before. Do you work at the (bookstore)?
>
> [*Pay a compliment*] That's a really nice shirt. Is blue your favorite color?

3 As you mix and mingle, write the names of your classmates in the spaces next to the questions.

Find someone who . . .

  1. has the same name as you   _____

  2. has the same birthday as you   _____

  3. was born in the same month as you   _____

  4. is from the same country as you   _____

  5. has been to (a specific place)   _____

  6. has three brothers   _____

  7. has only one brother or sister   _____

  8. has a pet   _____

  9. likes (a specific kind of food)   _____

 10. plays a musical instrument   _____

4 Discuss these questions in small groups.

1. Did you feel shy at the beginning of the activity?
2. Did you start to feel more comfortable after a few minutes? Why?
3. Did you find someone who shares your birthday or has the same name?
4. Which conversation starter do you like the best?
5. What did you talk about with your new classmates?
6. In general, how did you feel about the "mix and mingle" activity?

II. Presentation Preview

Your first presentation will be a speech about yourself. Speeches of self-introduction can help you and your classmates get to know one another.

ACTIVITY 1 Listen to a Model Speech

1 Read the information about the parts of a typical speech.

A typical speech has four parts. The *introduction* helps get your listeners' attention. It states your topic and includes a statement (called a *preview*) of what you will speak about in the body of the speech.

The *body* contains subtopics related to the main topic. Each subtopic is developed with facts, examples, reasons, or other kinds of details. The body is the longest part of your speech.

Transitions are words and phrases that separate the main parts of the speech. In the body of the speech, they also separate one subtopic from the next one. Very often transitions begin with words like "First," "Second," "Next," "Finally," and so on.

The *conclusion* includes a summary of your main ideas and provides final remarks to end your speech smoothly. The conclusion is also the place to thank your audience for listening.

2 Read and listen to Marina's model speech. Pay attention to each section of the speech and the details that she tells about herself. Notice the introduction, body, conclusion, and transitions.

Model Speech: About Me!

INTRODUCTION Good afternoon. My name is Marina, but all my friends call me Mari. I'd like to tell you a little bit about myself this afternoon.

Transition First, I'd like to tell you about my background.

BODY I was born in Brazil. I lived in Rio until I was thirteen years old. Then my family moved to Brasilia, the capital of Brazil. I lived with my parents and my four sisters.

Transition Second, I will tell you about my family.

My sister Ana is 8. My sister Sylvia is 9. My sister Claudia is 10. My sister Clarisse is 12. My parents and sisters are still in Brazil. My father owns a shoe store and my mother is a teacher.

Transition Next, I would like to tell you how I spend my time.

I go to school full time. My major is chemistry. My parents don't have money to *foot the bill* for my studies, so I had to get a part-time job and learn to *stand on my own*   * *Pay for*

(continued)

(Continued)

two feet. I have two part-time jobs. After school, I tutor high-school students in science. On Friday nights, I work at a Starbucks coffee shop.

* Be independent

Transition   Now let me tell you what I do when I have free time.

On the weekends, I like to go to the beach with my friends. When I have extra money, I love to shop for clothes. I also love to play the piano. I took lessons for ten years, so playing the piano is as *easy as pie* for me.

* Very easy

Transition   Finally, I want to tell you what my future plans are.

When I finish studying English, I want to return to Brazil and go to pharmacy school. I want to become a pharmacist. I also hope to get married some day and have three children. I would like to have two girls and a boy!

CONCLUSION   Now you know about my background, my family, my studies, my hobbies, and my plans for the future. Thank you for listening to my speech.

ACTIVITY 2   **Answer the Questions**

1 Listen again to the model speech. Then answer the following questions.

Questions	Answers
1. Where did Marina grow up?	_____
2. How many people are in Marina's family?	_____
3. What are her sisters' names?	_____
4. What is Marina's major?	_____
5. Where does Marina work?	_____
6. What does she do in her free time?	_____
7. What are her future plans?	_____

2 Work with a partner and compare answers.

ACTIVITY 3   **Discuss the Model Speech**

Discuss these questions in small groups.

1. What greeting did Mari use? What other information did she include in her introduction?
2. How many main topics did Mari discuss in the body of her speech? What were they?
3. Which words told you she was starting a new topic?
4. Which words signal that Mari was finished talking about her family?
5. What information did she include in her conclusion?
6. Was Mari's speech well organized? How do you know?
7. Did you like the speech? Why or why not?

III. Pronunciation Practice: [i] and [ɪ]

A common speaking error is to confuse the vowel sounds [i] (as in *bean*) and [ɪ] (as in *bin*). If you confuse these sounds, *it* sounds like *eat* and *sheep* sounds like *ship!*

The sound [i] is long and stressed. When you pronounce [i], spread your lips into a smile. Feel your lips stretching. In contrast, the sound [ɪ] is short and relaxed. When you pronounce [ɪ], your lips barely move.

ACTIVITY 1 **Contrast Words and Sentences with [i] and [ɪ]**

Listen and repeat the following sets of words and sentences with [i] and [ɪ].

[i]	[ɪ]
1. feet	fit
2. sheep	ship
3. team	Tim
4. seek	sick
5. heat	hit
6. She will leave.	She will live.
7. Did he sleep?	Did he slip?
8. Can you feel it?	Can you fill it?
9. Change the wheel.	Change the will.
10. He made a feast.	He made a fist.

> **PRONUNCIATION TIP**
> - The letters *ee, ei,* and *ie* are usually pronounced [i].
> - Examples: s<u>ee</u>, fr<u>ee</u>dom, rec<u>ei</u>ve, p<u>ie</u>ce, gr<u>ie</u>f

ACTIVITY 2 **Practice Sentences from the Model Speech**

Listen and repeat the following sentences from Marina's speech. Be sure to pronounce the [i] and [ɪ] words correctly.

    [ɪ]   [ɪ] [i]   [i]
1. I l<u>i</u>ved <u>i</u>n R<u>i</u>o until I was thirt<u>ee</u>n.

         [ɪ]   [ɪ] [ɪ]   [ɪ]
2. My s<u>i</u>sters are st<u>ill</u> <u>i</u>n Braz<u>i</u>l.

  [ɪ]   [i]
3. <u>I</u>t's as <u>ea</u>sy as pie.

        [i]   [i]
4. On the w<u>ee</u>kends, I go to the b<u>ea</u>ch.

         [ɪ]   [i]
5. Thank you for l<u>i</u>stening to my sp<u>ee</u>ch.

ACTIVITY 3 **Practice the Model Speech**

1 Listen to the speech on page 3 again. Circle the words pronounced with [i] and underline the words with [ɪ].

2 Work with a partner. Take turns reading Marina's speech aloud. Pay attention to your pronunciation of [i] and [ɪ]. (Remember, you should "smile" as you say [i]. Your lips should hardly move as you pronounce [ɪ].)

IV. Playing with Sayings: Sayings with [i] and [ɪ]

ACTIVITY 1 Learn the Meanings

1 Read the following sayings and their meanings. Check (✓) the ones you heard in Marina's model speech on page 3. Refer back to the speech if necessary.

_____ 1. **as easy as pie:** very simple or easy to do
Playing the piano is *as easy as pie* for me.

_____ 2. **like sardines (in a can):** very crowded; no room to move
In Tokyo, passengers pack into the subway *like sardines*.

_____ 3. **foot the bill:** to pay the expenses
My father is *footing the bill* for my education.

_____ 4. **stand on one's own two feet:** to be independent or responsible for one's own life
Now that you are twenty-one, you should *stand on your own two feet*.

_____ 5. **seeing is believing:** personally seeing an event makes it easier to believe
than only reading or hearing about it
I didn't believe how beautiful the baby was until I saw her in person.
Seeing is believing!

2 Circle the [i] sounds in the sayings in Activity 1. Underline the [ɪ] sounds. Say the words with these sounds. Then pronounce each saying out loud several times.

ACTIVITY 2 Use the Sayings

1 Work in small groups. Unscramble the sayings and write them correctly.

a. It's time to (*on your two own feet stand*) _____ and get a job.

b. His uncle is willing to (*the bill foot*) _____ and buy him a new suit.

c. When we were in the crowded elevator, we felt (*like in a sardines can*).
_____

d. You can learn this card trick. It's (*as pie as easy*) _____!

e. I didn't understand how hot it is in the Amazon until I went there. (*believing is*

    seeing)!_____

2 Take turns reading the sentences. Be sure to pronounce [i] and [ɪ] correctly.

V. Presentation Project: About Me!

Your first project is to present a two- to three-minute speech about yourself. You will use one of these two methods for planning and preparing your About Me speech:

- brainstorming balloons
- photo story

Method A: Brainstorming Balloons

In this method you will use a visual aid called *brainstorming balloons* to take notes for your speech. Later you will write those notes on index cards. A quick look at the index cards while you are giving your speech will remind you of what to say.

A Look at Marina's brainstorming balloons. Where is the speech title? What are the five topics in the body of the speech? What details does she give about her family?

Marina's Brainstorming Balloons Worksheet

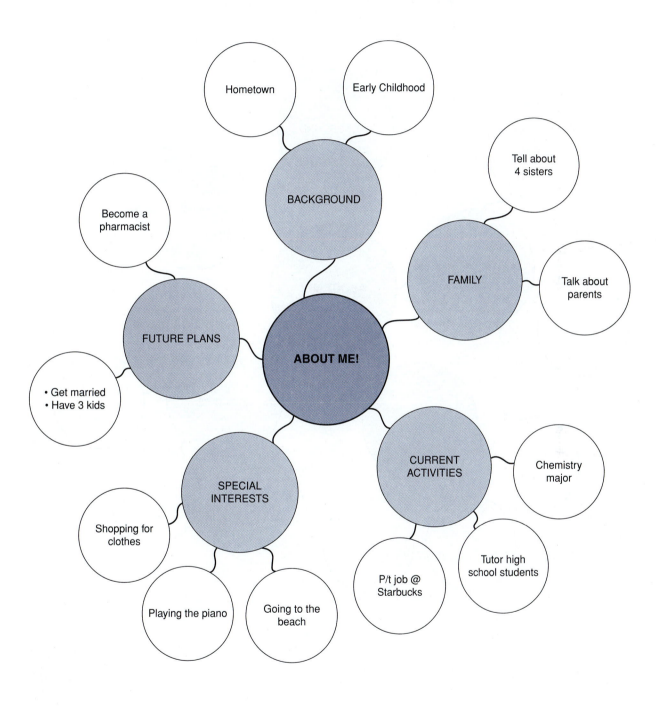

B Now complete your own brainstorming balloons Worksheet to prepare for your speech.
Add more balloons if you need them.

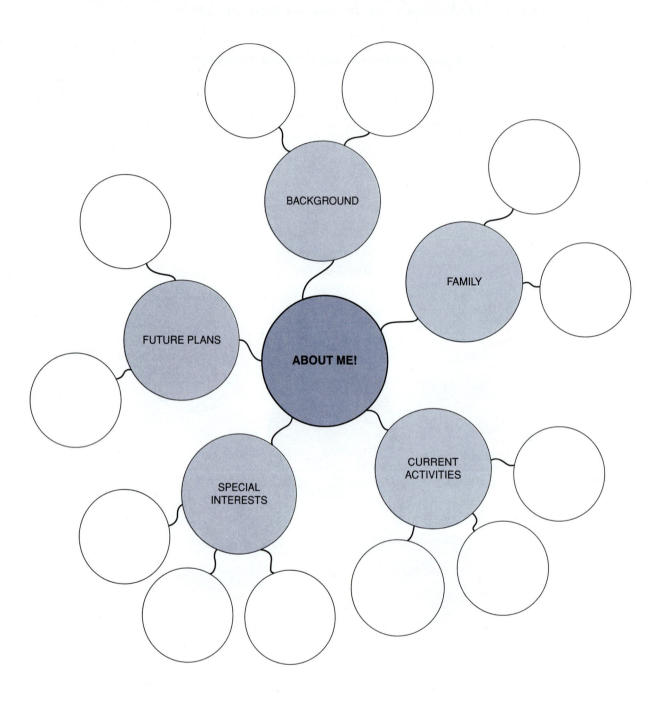

C Read the instructions for organizing your speech.

Introduction
1. Greet the audience.
2. Introduce yourself by name.

Body
Include information about these topics:
1. Background (hometown, childhood)
2. Family
3. Current activities (school, work)
4. Hobbies and interests
5. Future plans

Conclusion
1. Summarize the topics you spoke about.
2. Thank the audience for listening.

D Read the Useful Language expressions you can use to begin and end your speech. Place a checkmark (✓) next to the expressions you like best.

USEFUL LANGUAGE: BEGINNING YOUR SPEECH

_____ Good morning/afternoon *or* Hi everyone!

_____ Today I am going to tell you about myself.

_____ I'd like to introduce myself.

_____ My name is . . .

_____ My friends call me . . .

USEFUL LANGUAGE: CONCLUDING YOUR SPEECH

_____ I hope you liked hearing about my background, family, activities, special interests, and future dreams.

_____ Thank you so much for listening to my speech.

_____ Thank you for being such a great audience.

E Select a saying from page 6 to include in your speech. Write it here: _____
Decide where and how you will use it.

STEP 2 | Prepare Note Cards

Write the details from your brainstorming balloons on note cards. Use at least seven cards. Label and number them as shown in the examples below.

INTRODUCTION   1

Greeting: Good afternoon.

Introduce myself:
-My name is Marina but all my friends call me Mari.
- I'd like to tell you a little about myself this
    afternoon.

MY BACKGROUND   2

Hometown: Rio, Brazil until 13 years old
Early childhood: Moved to Brasilia
Other details: Lived with parents and
    four sisters

MY FAMILY   3

Parents: Live in Brazil; father owns shoe store;
    mother is a teacher

Sisters: Ana is 8; Sylvia is 9; Claudia is 10;
    Clarisse is 12

CURRENT ACTIVITIES   4

Major: Chemistry
Parents don't have money to [idiom] *foot the
    bills. . . . I had to learn to* [idiom] *stand on my own
    two feet*
Jobs: tutor high school students in science;
    Starbucks coffee shop on Friday nights

SPECIAL INTERESTS   5

Special talents: play the piano; lessons for
    10 years; [idiom]
    It is as easy as pie for me.

Favorite things to do: go to the
    beach; shop for clothes

FUTURE PLANS 6

Educational: Return to Brazil for pharmacy school

Professional: Become a pharmacist

Personal: Get married, have two girls
    and a boy

CONCLUSION 7

Summary: Now you know about my background, my
    family, my studies, my hobbies, and my plans
    for the future.

Thank audience: Thank you for listening to my
    speech.

STEP 3 | Practice Your Speech

A Practice your speech in front of a mirror using your note cards. Record it and listen to it at least once. Make sure the speech is two to three minutes long.

B Complete the Speech Checklist. Is there anything you want to improve before you present your speech in class?

Speech Checklist	YES	NO
1. I included an introduction with a greeting.	❑	❑
2. I included five sections in the body of the speech.	❑	❑
3. My conclusion included a summary.	❑	❑
4. I thanked the audience for listening to my speech.	❑	❑
5. I included a saying from the chapter.	❑	❑
6. I included one or more Useful Language expressions.	❑	❑
7. My speech is two to three minutes long.	❑	❑
8. My pronunciation of words with [i] and [ɪ] is clear.	❑	❑

C Practice again with your note cards.

D Your teacher and/or your classmates may evaluate your speech. Study the form on page 139 so you know how you will be evaluated. You may use the items on the form to make final changes to your speech.

STEP 4 | Present Your Speech

A Relax, take a deep breath, and present your speech.

B Listen to your audience's applause.

Method B: Photo Story Speech

With this method, your goal is to use three photographs to assist you as you prepare and present your speech. Instead of note cards, your photos will help you remember what to say.

STEP 1 | Plan Your Speech

A Look through your photo albums or digital photos saved on your computer. Choose three that represent:

- your childhood
- your current activities
- your future plans

B Study the examples. Do you think the photos are effective? Why or why not?

Rahul's Childhood

This is my first photo. It reminds me of my childhood in India because my parents trained elephants. We lived in a village about an hour from New Delhi. I have a twin sister named Indira. When we were two years old, my father gave us our first ride on an elephant. He wanted us to be comfortable around these wonderful animals.

Monique's Current Activities

I don't have much free time because I am taking five classes. They are Art History, Psychology, Algebra, Music Appreciation, and Speech. When I am not in school, I work at a movie theatre selling soft drinks and popcorn. But when I do have free time, my second photo shows that I love to play the piano.

Cesar's Future Plans

My last photo is of my horse, Regalo. *Regalo* means "gift" in Spanish. I took this picture last month. It represents my future because I hope to become a large-animal veterinarian. I want to return to my country, Honduras, and take care of the horses and cows on my father's cattle ranch in the countryside.

C Read the Useful Language expressions you can use to introduce your photos. Place a checkmark (✓) next to the expressions you like best.

> **USEFUL LANGUAGE: INTRODUCING YOUR PHOTOS**
>
> _____ This is my first photo. It reminds me of my childhood because . . .
>
> _____ This is my second photo. It shows [me] . . .
>
> _____ And now for my last photo! It shows . . .
>
> _____ My third and final photo shows . . . It represents my future because . . .

D Read the following guidelines for organizing your speech.

Introduction
   1. Greet the audience.
   2. Introduce yourself by name.

Body
   1. Show your first photo. Describe how it represents your past.
   2. Show your second photo. Describe how it represents your present life.
   3. Show your third photo. Describe how it represents your future.

Conclusion
   1. Summarize the areas you spoke about.
   2. Thank the audience for listening.

STEP 2 | Practice Your Speech

A Practice your speech in front of a mirror using your note cards. Record it and listen to it at least once. Make sure the speech is two to three minutes long.

B Complete the Speech Checklist. Is there anything you want to improve before you present your speech in class?

Speech Checklist	YES	NO
1. I included an introduction with a greeting.	❑	❑
2. I chose three photos representing my life.	❑	❑
3. My photos are large enough for everyone to see.	❑	❑
4. I included details about my past, present, and future plans.	❑	❑
5. I included a saying from the chapter.	❑	❑
6. My conclusion included a summary.	❑	❑
7. I thanked the audience for listening to my speech.	❑	❑
8. I included one or more Useful Language expressions.	❑	❑
9. My pronunciation of words with [i] and [ɪ] is clear.	❑	❑
10. My speech is two to three minutes long.	❑	❑

C Practice again.

D Your teacher and/or your classmates may evaluate your speech. Study the form on page 141 so you know how you will be evaluated. You may use the checklist to make final changes to your speech.

STEP 3 | Present Your Speech

A Relax, take a deep breath, and present your speech.

B Listen to your audience's applause.

CHAPTER 2

EFFECTIVE SPEECH DELIVERY

A speech is more than just the words you use. *How* you say something is just as important as *what* you say! Good delivery involves several important elements. First, you must practice. Second, it is important to be yourself. Finally, think of your listeners as your new friends; look at them, smile, gesture, and speak to them the way you do in everyday conversation with old friends.

CHAPTER CHALLENGE Your challenge in this chapter is to learn tips for delivering a speech in front of an audience. By the time you complete this chapter you will be able to:

- maintain eye contact with your audience
- use appropriate gestures
- plan, prepare, and present a speech about a meaningful object

I. Eye Contact

When speaking to groups of people, large or small, try to look at all of your listeners directly. If you look at the floor, at the corners of the room, or over people's heads, your audience will think you are not interested in them or in your topic. Remember to look at your entire audience, not just the teacher or a few selected people.

ACTIVITY Practice Eye Contact

1 **Work in groups of four or five classmates. Move your chairs into a circle.**

   a. Take turns describing what you did last weekend. Each person should speak for one to two minutes.

   b. As you speak, look directly at one classmate for two or three seconds; then move your eyes to the next person and do the same. Continue looking at each member of your group, one at a time, until you finish speaking.

2 **Discuss these questions as a class:**

   a. Did you feel comfortable when you looked directly at your classmates? Why or why not?

   b. Did you ever look away? Where did you look?

   c. Did your classmates look at you while you were speaking? How did that make you feel?

   d. How could the listeners have helped you to feel more comfortable?

3 **Repeat the activity with different classmates. This time discuss your plans for next weekend. Don't break eye contact with your listeners!**

II. Posture

Posture is the way you stand in front of your audience. Good posture makes you appear confident and reliable. To achieve good posture, stand up straight and keep your head up, with your chin parallel to the floor. If you are using a lectern or speaker's stand, be sure not to lean on it or bend over it. Instead, stand tall and rest your hands on the sides of the lectern gently.

ACTIVITY Practice Good Posture

1 **Stand next to your chair. Gently place this book on your head.**

2 **Count to ten slowly. Keep the book balanced on your head.**

3 **Try it again. This time count to twenty.**

4 **Walk slowly around the classroom with the book on your head. If it starts to slide off, put it back and keep walking until your teacher tells you to stop.**

III. Gestures

Gestures are your hand and arm movements. Speakers use them to emphasize important points or to describe things. Your use of gestures can help your listeners understand your speech better.

EXAMPLES OF MEANINGFUL GESTURES

To demonstrate size: Use your hands to show how wide or tall an object is.

To show location: Point with your index finger. Sweep your hand from side to side to show east-to-west direction.

To emphasize numbers: Hold up two fingers as you say, "There are *two* types of ..."

To say yes or to illustrate something positive: Nod your head up and down.

To say no or to illustrate something negative: Shake your head from side to side.

To make words come alive: Act out the action that you are talking about.
For example:

- Shrug your shoulders if you say something is confusing.
- Hold your index finger in front of your lips if you describe a quiet situation.
- Pretend to lift a spoon to your mouth if you are talking about someone eating.
- Touch your finger to your nose if you describe how something smells.

Gestures add color and interest to your speech. In contrast, you should avoid movements that are unnecessary or distracting. For example:

- moving your hair off your face or out of your eyes
- pushing your glasses up on your nose
- playing with a pen or piece of jewelry you are wearing
- folding and unfolding your arms
- rocking or moving from side to side

Express Messages Nonverbally

1 Work in groups of four or five. Use gestures to express the following messages. Don't speak!

I'm confused.	It's hot in here.	I'm tired.
Stop!	No, I don't agree.	Talking on the phone.
I'm cold.	Yes, I agree.	I don't know.
Come here.	Good luck!	Calm down.
I don't feel well.	It's time to leave.	I'm in love.
Wait a minute.	He's crazy.	She's very smart.

2 Discuss the following questions with the class.

    a. Did the members of your group use different gestures to express the same message?

    b. How would North Americans express these messages with gestures?

ACTIVITY 2 **Analyze Gestures**

1 Work with a partner. Study the gestures shown in the pictures and discuss the questions.

    a. How do you interpret the gesture in each illustration?

    b. Did you and your partner interpret any of the gestures differently? How?

2 Discuss your responses with the class.

IV. Presentation Preview

Your goal for this chapter is to choose an object that has very special meaning for you and prepare a speech about it. You will describe the object and explain why it is important to you. The speech should be two to three minutes long.

ACTIVITY 1 Listen to a Model Speech

Listen to Olga's speech about a meaningful object. Pay attention to her organization and use of details.

Model Speech: My Grandfather's Lucky Lighter

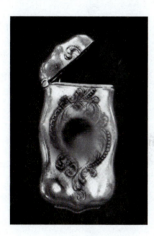

INTRODUCTION In my hand I have an object that saved my grandfather's life. Without this object, my father, my brothers, and I would not be here. Can you see what it is? It is a cigarette lighter.

BODY

Facts about the Object This cigarette lighter is from Budapest, Hungary. It is a rectangle about two inches by three inches. It weighs about four ounces. It is made of silver. It used to be shiny but now it is dull. It has lots of scratches and a big dent. It is more than seventy years old.

My grandfather got it when he was sixteen. He had just started smoking. One day he was riding his bike, and some robbers started shooting guns in the street. A bullet hit him in his shirt pocket, in the exact place where he kept his lighter. The bullet bounced off the lighter. And that's how the lighter saved my grandfather's life.

My grandfather brought the "lucky lighter" to the hospital on the day I was born nineteen years ago. He gave it to me because he wanted me to be as lucky in life as he was.

Feelings about the Object When I was young, I didn't understand how important the lighter was. I feel strongly about it now because it reminds me of my grandfather's love and the many lessons he taught me. For instance, he taught me to tell the truth and to *lend a hand* when someone needs help.   * *Help*

CONCLUSION I hope you now understand why this old, dull object has special meaning for me. Without it, I wouldn't be here today. We should all remember how lucky we are to be here. Life can be short.

Thank you, everyone, for listening to my speech.

🎧 **1 Listen to Olga's speech again. Complete the worksheet with information from her speech.**

Olga's Speech Preparation Worksheet: Meaningful Object

INTRODUCTION

Object saved grandfather's life. What is it? Lighter.

BODY

Facts about the Object

1. Where is it from?	
2. What are its features (for example, shape, size, weight, color, material)?	
3. How old is it?	
4. What is the history of the object?	
5. When, where, and why did Olga get it?	
6. Why does it have special meaning for her?	

Feelings about the Object

CONCLUSION

Without object I wouldn't be here. We should all remember how lucky we are. Thank you.

2 Compare answers with a partner.

ACTIVITY 3 Model Speech Discussion

Discuss these questions in small groups.

1. What did Olga say to get her listeners' attention in the first sentence?
2. What facts did she give about her object?
3. What are Olga's feelings now about her object?
4. How did she conclude her speech?
5. What makes objects meaningful to their owners?
6. Do meaningful objects have to be worth a lot of money? Explain.

V. Pronunciation Practice: Final Consonant Sounds

Many English learners drop or forget to pronounce final consonants. If you do this, your listeners may have difficulty understanding you. Be sure to pronounce final consonants clearly.

EXAMPLES:

ca**ke** (the last sound is [k])   bi**te** (the last sound is [t])   ro**de** (the last sound is [d])

ACTIVITY 1 Practice Word Contrasts

Listen and repeat the sentences. Exaggerate your pronunciation of the underlined final consonants.

1. I los**t** my ca**ne.**   I los**t** my ca**pe.**
2. He wro**te** i**t.**   He ro**de** i**t.**
3. My ca**t** is fi**ne.**   My ca**t** is fi**ve.**
4. I ca**n** go.   I ca**n't** go.
5. He'**s** not dea**d.**   He'**s** not dea**f.**

ACTIVITY 2 Practice Sentences

Listen and repeat the sentences from Olga's speech. Be sure to pronounce the underlined final consonants clearly.

1. I**n** my han**d**, I ha**ve** a**n** obje**ct.**
2. I**t** i**s** more tha**n** seventy year**s** ol**d.**
3. A bulle**t** hi**t** hi**m** i**n** hi**s** shir**t** pocke**t.**
4. Life ca**n** be shor**t.**
5. I hope you now understand why this old, dull object has special meaning for me.

ACTIVITY 3 Practice the Model Speech

Work with a partner. Take turns reading Olga's speech aloud. Pay attention to your pronunciation of final consonants.

VI. Playing with Sayings: Sayings with Final Consonants

ACTIVITY 1 Learn the Meanings

Read the following sayings. Place a checkmark [✓] next to the ones you heard in Olga's model speech on page 19. Refer back to the speech if necessary.

_____ 1. **in over one's head:** to do something or be in a situation that is too difficult
Stella can't understand the chapter. She's *in over her head.*

_____ 2. **lose one's head:** to act without thinking
After my boss gave me a small raise, I *lost my head* and bought an expensive car.

_____ 3. **out of hand:** disorganized, out of control
The meeting *got out of hand* when everyone began to shout.

_____ 4. **lend a hand:** to provide help
Would you *lend a hand* and help me fix my flat tire?

_____ 5. **one's heart isn't in it:** one is not interested in or enthusiastic about something
I don't want to do housework today. My *heart isn't in it.*

1 **Work in small groups. Read the following sentences and circle the answer choice that has the same meaning.**

a. Marilyn's spending is *getting out of hand.*

1. Something fell out of her hand.

2. She burned her hand.

3. She spends too much money.

b. Ali is *in over his head* at work.

1. He is underwater.

2. He has too much work.

3. He is very short.

c. Ezra offered to *lend his mother a hand* in the kitchen.

1. Ezra refused to cook dinner.

2. Ezra helped his mother.

3. Ezra is in the kitchen.

d. I'm not going to the birthday party. My *heart's not in it.*

1. I don't like to go to parties.

2. I don't know the other guests very well.

3. I'm not interested in attending the party.

e. Everything was half price. Margo *lost her head* and spent $1,000.

1. She spent too much money.

2. She lost her hat in the store and went to the lost and found.

3. She lost her sense of direction and couldn't find the exit.

2 **Fill in the blanks with the correct saying.**

a. I asked my friend to _____lend a hand_____ and help me carry the heavy box.

b. The children got _____ and started throwing things out the window.

c. I had a disagreement with my mom. Later she asked me to go shopping with her, but _____.

d. He liked the tie so much that he _____ and bought one in every color.

e. I am _____. It was a mistake to take seven classes.

3 **With a partner, practice reading the sentences aloud. Be sure to pronounce final consonant sounds clearly.**

VII. Presentation Project: A Meaningful Object

Your project is to prepare and present a speech about an object that has special meaning to you. You will need to bring your object to class to show your classmates.

STEP 1 | Choose an Object

Choose an object that is very special to you. For example:

a painting or photo	a souvenir from a trip	a document
a piece of clothing	a lock of hair	an antique
a household object	a piece of jewelry	a book

A Fill in the Speech Preparation Worksheet. You may change some questions or add your own. Use Olga's Speech Preparation Worksheet, page 20, as a model.

Speech Preparation Worksheet: Meaningful Object

INTRODUCTION

BODY

Facts about the Object

1. Where is it from?

2. What are its features (for example, shape, size, weight, color, material)?

3. How old is it?

4. What is the history of the object?

5. When, where, and why did you get it?

Feelings about the Object

6. Why does it have special meaning for you?

CONCLUSION

B Read the Useful Language expressions for getting your listeners' attention. Place a checkmark (✓) next to the expressions you like best.

USEFUL LANGUAGE: GETTING LISTENERS' ATTENTION

_____ In my hand I have a very special object.

_____ I have a special object to share with you today. It is a _____.

_____ Behind my back I am holding a very special object. Would you like to know what it is?

C Select a saying from pages 21 to include in your speech. Write it here:

_____. Decide where and how you will use it.

D Read the following guidelines for organizing your speech.

> **Introduction**
> 1. Get your listeners' attention with your first statement. Try to make your audience curious about what you will say next.
> 2. Tell your audience what your object is.
>
> **Body**
> 1. Provide facts about your object. Include as many details as possible.
> 2. Describe your feelings about your object.
> 3. Say why this object has special meaning for you.
>
> **Conclusion**
> 1. Make a final statement your audience will remember.
> 2. Thank your audience for listening to you.

STEP 3 | Prepare Note Cards

A Label the cards as follows:

- Introduction
- Facts about the Object
- Feelings about the Object
- Conclusion

B Fill in the information from your Speech Preparation Worksheet. Use as many cards as you need.

C Write the Useful Language expression and the saying you selected on your note cards.

D Organize the cards according to the instructions above. Number your cards.

STEP 4 | Add Meaningful Gestures

A In the following chart, write gestures and facial expressions that you could use in your speech.

Place in Speech	Gesture
EXAMPLE: Olga said a bullet hit the lighter in her grandfather's pocket.	**EXAMPLE:** She tapped the pocket area on her blouse with her index finger.

B Add reminders about the gestures to your note cards.

STEP 5 | Practice Your Speech

A Practice your speech in front of a mirror using your note cards. Record it and listen to it at least once. Make sure it is two to three minutes long.

B Complete the Speech Checklist. Is there anything you want to improve before you present your speech in class?

Speech Checklist	YES	NO
1. I got my listeners' attention with a Useful Language expression.	☐	☐
2. I named my object.	☐	☐
3. I included facts about the object.	☐	☐
4. I included my feelings about the object.	☐	☐
5. I included a conclusion and thanked the audience for listening.	☐	☐
6. I included a saying.	☐	☐
7. I used meaningful gestures.	☐	☐
8. My posture and eye contact were effective.	☐	☐
9. My pronunciation of final consonant sounds was clear.	☐	☐
10. My speech is two to three minutes long.	☐	☐

C Practice one or two more times using your note cards.

D Your teacher and/or your classmates may evaluate your speech. Study the form on page 141 so you know how you will be evaluated. You may use the items on the form to make final changes to your speech.

STEP 6 | Practice Your Speech in Small Groups

A Work in groups of four or five. Sit in a circle.

B Give your speech from your seat. Then listen to your classmates' speeches and time them.

C Give your classmates feedback. Include:
- what you liked about their speeches
- suggestions for improvement

STEP 7 | Present Your Speech

A Relax, take a deep breath and present your speech. As you speak, remember to stand tall, make eye contact, and use meaningful gestures.

B Listen to your audience's applause!

CHAPTER 3

DON'T JUST TELL ME, SHOW ME!

Good speakers know that "telling isn't everything." When you tell listeners information, they will remember some of it. But if you tell them *and* show them, they will remember much more of what you say.

Audiences enjoy eye-catching, colorful visuals or other memorable speech aids. Great speech aids help listeners to understand and remember your speech.

CHAPTER CHALLENGE: Your challenge in this chapter is to choose speech aids that keep your audience interested during your speech. This chapter has many examples and ideas to help you select speech aids. By the time you complete this chapter, you will be able to:

- identify the most popular types of speech aids
- use speech aids effectively
- plan, prepare, and present a speech about something you fear

I. The Five Senses

Audiences learn far more when a speaker presents information in more than one way. Good speakers can reach listeners through hearing, seeing, touching, smelling, and even tasting, as the following examples show.

Hearing

In a speech about Amazon jungle parrots, Pablo played a recording of the screeches and squawks that the parrots use to communicate.

Taste

In a speech about tea in India, Pari had samples of tea for the listeners to taste.

Smell

In a speech about aromatherapy as a treatment for depression, Lili provided small vials of lavender and vanilla extract for the audience to smell.

Touch

In a speech about origami, the Japanese art of paper folding, Kimiko taught the class how to fold paper into the form of a little bird.

Sight

In a speech about New York City, Tariq showed a two-foot-high model of the Statue of Liberty.

TYPES OF VISUAL AIDS

Sketches or Diagrams
This diagram shows how computers are linked in a network.

Graph
This graph shows percentages of English speakers around the world.

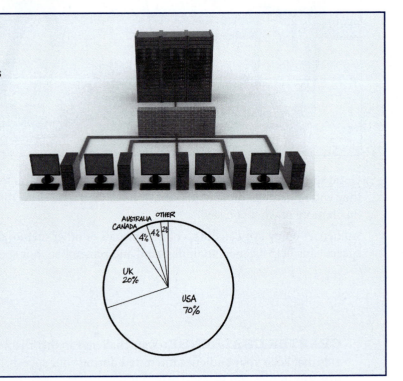

Maps

This map shows the countries that border on Brazil.

Photographs

This is a photo of an English bulldog.

Physical Objects

This is a calligraphy pen.

Models of Objects

This is a model of the Eiffel Tower.

1 Work with a partner. Read the items. Write *Yes* in the space if something is a good idea. Write *No* if it is a bad idea.

_____ a. Face your visual aid, not the audience.

_____ b. Make objects large enough for everyone to see.

_____ c. Pass out papers during your speech.

_____ d. Face your audience when referring to your visual aid.

_____ e. Discuss visual aids one at a time.

_____ f. Keep visual aids simple.

_____ g. Present all of your visual aids at the same time.

_____ h. Pass around small photos for all to see during your speech.

2 Can you think of any other things you should and should not do when you use visual aids? Make a list.

3 Share your responses with the class.

ACTIVITY 2 Select Speech Aids

1 Work in small groups. Read the speech topics. Fill in the blanks with speech aids that the speakers could use during their presentations.

EXAMPLE:

Fernanda gave a speech to convince her listeners to install smoke detectors in every room of their house.

Photos: <u>photos of a home destroyed by fire</u>

Sound: <u>recorded sound of a fire alarm going off</u>

Object: <u>actual smoke detector</u>

Graph: <u>graph showing numbers of people whose lives were saved by smoke detectors</u>

a. Mila gave a speech to convince her listeners to wear their seatbelts whenever they are in a car.

Photo: _____

Sound: _____

Graph: _____

Other: _____

b. Paolo gave a speech about the health benefits of eating honey.

Object: _____

Taste: _____

Photo: _____

Other: _____

c. Lucas demonstrated the different ways to use sandpaper.

Touch: _____

Sketch: _____

Photo: _____

Other: _____

   d. Eva talked about three different types of coffee beans.

     Object: _____

     Taste: _____

     Smell: _____

     Other: _____

   e. Suri gave a speech about her pet snake.

     Touch: _____

     Photo: _____

     Object: _____

     Other: _____

2 Share your ideas with the rest of the class.

II. Presentation Preview

Your goal in this chapter is to choose something you are afraid of and to prepare a speech about it. Everyone is afraid of something! Talking about a fear is a good way to gain confidence when you speak before an audience.

ACTIVITY 1 Listen to a Model Presentation

 Listen to a model speech about Humberto's fear of flying in small planes.

MODEL SPEECH: My Fear of Flying

INTRODUCTION   I didn't want to die! So *I crossed my fingers* and prayed. It was my first time flying in a small airplane. The weather was very bad. Suddenly, the engine of the plane stopped!

       * Hoped for good luck*

Statement of fear   This was the beginning of my great fear of flying in small planes.

Humberto showed a picture of a small plane.

BODY   My fear developed last year. I was flying from Cancun to the island of Cozumel in the Yucatan, Mexico. Let me show you exactly where I was at the time.

(continued)

(Continued)

Right after we took off from the airport in Cancun, the weather became very bad. There was a lot of thunder and lightning. It began to rain very hard. The pilot couldn't even see out of the windows of the plane. I was the only other person in the plane.

Humberto showed a map of the Yucatan Peninsula.

After about fifteen minutes in the air, the plane started to shake and make strange noises. Then the engine stopped! It was so scary! I began to tremble and sweat. I felt like I was in a paper airplane like this one:

I remember thinking, "I'm too young to die!" But the pilot stayed calm, and that *lifted my spirits* a little. All of a sudden the engine started again. The pilot turned to me with a big smile and said, "¡No te preocupes!" (That means "Don't worry!") Finally, we landed in Cozumel. I celebrated being alive by buying the largest ice cream cone I could find. It *melted in my mouth*!

* *Made me feel better*

* *Was delicious*

CONCLUSION Now you know why I am afraid of flying in small planes. It makes me upset just to think about this experience. I'm sure I will never overcome it. I know that I will never fly in a small plane again. Thank you all for listening to my speech.

ACTIVITY 2 **Complete the Statements**

1 Listen to Humberto's speech again and fill in the blanks with the correct words.

a. Humberto is very afraid of (*verb*) <u>flying</u> in (*adjective*) <u>small</u> (*plural noun*) <u>planes.</u>

b. Humberto started his flight at the (*compound noun*) _____ in Cancun.

c. He was going to (*proper noun*) _____.

d. The (*noun*) _____ was very bad.

e. It began to (*verb*) _____ very hard. The pilot couldn't (*verb*) _____ out the (*plural noun*) _____.

f. After (*number*) _____ minutes, the plane (*past-tense verb*) _____ to shake and make (*adjective*) _____ noises.

g. Then the engine (*past-tense verb*) _____ !

h. Humberto began to tremble and (*verb*) _____.

i. He thought, "I'm too young to (*verb*) _____." But the pilot stayed (*adjective*) _____.

j. All of a sudden the (*noun*) _____ (*past-tense verb*) _____ again.

k. The pilot (*past-tense verb*) _____ to Humberto and (*past-tense verb*) _____, "¡No te preocupes!"

l. They finally (*past-tense verb*) _____ in (*proper noun*) _____.

m. Humberto (*past-tense verb*) _____ being alive.

n. Humberto's ice cream (*past-tense verb*) _____ in his (*noun*) _____.

2 Work with a partner and compare answers.

ACTIVITY 3 Model Speech Discussion

Discuss these questions in small groups.

1. Did Humberto's introduction get your attention? How?
2. What is Humberto's fear?
3. What caused Humberto's fear? What details did he give about this?
4. How did he feel at the time?
5. Did the story have a happy or a sad ending?
6. What did Humberto say in his conclusion? Was this an effective way to end the speech?
7. How many speech aids did Humberto use? How did they improve his speech?
8. What other types of speech aids could he have used?

III. Pronunciation Practice: Regular Past-Tense Verbs

The *-ed* ending that forms regular past-tense verbs in English can have three different pronunciations: [t], [d], and the new syllable [əd].

- When the last sound in the past-tense verb is voiceless (with no vibration in the throat), such as [p], [s], [k], or [f], the *-ed* ending will sound like [t]. For example:
  walk**ed** finish**ed** kiss**ed** stopp**ed**

- When the last sound in the past-tense verb is voiced (with vibration in the throat), like [b], [g], [n], or any vowel, the *-ed* ending will sound like [d]. For example:
  phon**ed** liv**ed** call**ed** play**ed**

- When the last sound in the past-tense verb is either [t] or [d], the *-ed* ending will sound like the new syllable [əd]. For example:
  paint**ed** need**ed**

ACTIVITY 1 Practice Saying *-ed* Like [t]

Listen and repeat the verb pairs and sentences. Be sure to pronounce *-ed* as [t].

Present-Tense Verbs	Past-Tense Verbs	Sentences
1. look	looked	6. She baked a pie.
2. miss	missed	7. Papa kissed the baby.
3. stop	stopped	8. Orlando stopped working.
4. work	worked	9. The children picked flowers.
5. laugh	laughed	10. Katia crossed the street.

ACTIVITY 2 Practice Saying *-ed* Like [d]

Listen and repeat the verb pairs and sentences. Be sure to pronounce *-ed* as [d].

Present-Tense Verbs	Past-Tense Verbs	Sentences
1. hug	hugged	6. I filled the glass.
2. climb	climbed	7. We stayed out late.
3. clean	cleaned	8. He turned the handle.
4. move	moved	9. They loved the movie.
5. follow	followed	10. Kiko cried like a baby.

ACTIVITY 3 Practice Saying *-ed* Like the New Syllable [əd]

Listen and repeat the verb pairs and sentences. Be sure to pronounce *-ed* as the new syllable [əd].

Present-Tense Verbs	Past-Tense Verbs	Sentences
1. paint	painted	6. He avoided his boss.
2. fade	faded	7. I rested at home.
3. need	needed	8. The car started.
4. add	added	9. Mike needed money.
5. want	wanted	10. We waited for a taxi.

ACTIVITY 4 Identify Regular Past-Tense Verbs

1 Listen to Humberto's model speech again as you look at pages 31 and 32. Circle eleven regular past-tense verbs. Write the verbs in the chart below. The first two appear as examples.

-ed = [t]	*-ed* = [d]	*-ed* = [əd]
crossed	prayed	

2 Take turns pronouncing the lists of words with a partner.

ACTIVITY 5 Practice the Model Speech

Now take turns reading the model speech on pages 31–32 aloud with your partner. Be sure to pronounce the past-tense verbs correctly.

IV. Playing with Sayings: Sayings with Regular Past-Tense Verbs

ACTIVITY 1 Learn the Meanings

1 Read the following sayings and their meanings. Place a checkmark (✓) next to the ones you heard in Humberto's model speech. Refer back to the speech if necessary.

_____ a. **save the day:** to rescue; to act in a way that prevents a bad ending
When I spilled juice on my shirt, my friend *saved the day* and loaned me a clean one.

_____ b. **cross one's fingers:** to hope for the best; to wish for good luck
She *crossed her fingers* that she would win the prize.

_____ c. **count one's blessings:** to be grateful for one's good luck
When I fell off my bike, I *counted my blessings* that I didn't get hurt.

_____ d. **melt in one's mouth:** to taste wonderful; to be delicious
My mother baked an apple pie that *melted in my mouth.*

_____ e. **lift one's spirits:** to feel better; to feel happy
My best friend *lifted my spirits* when she invited me to lunch.

2 Circle all the regular past-tense verbs in the sentences above.

3 List the verbs you circled.

-ed = [t]	*-ed* = [d]	*-ed* = [əd]

4 Work with a partner. Pronounce each verb in the chart several times.

ACTIVITY 2 **Use the Sayings**

1 Work in small groups. Unscramble the sayings and write the words in the correct order.

a. My son (*his blessings counted*) _____ when he passed all of his exams.

b. The brownie I had for dessert just (*in mouth my melted*) _____.

c. He (*fingers his crossed*) _____ that his car wouldn't break down.

d. My neighbor (*day the saved*) _____ by giving me a ride when my car broke down.

e. When I was sick, my favorite music (*my lifted spirits*) _____.

2 Take turns reading the sentences aloud to each other. Be sure to pronounce the past-tense verbs correctly.

V. Presentation Project: My Worst Fear

Your project is to prepare and present a two- to three-minute speech about something you fear. You might be surprised to learn that others are afraid of the same thing as you! Follow these steps to prepare your speech.

STEP 1 | Choose a Topic

Here are some examples of common fears. You may choose one of these topics or pick your own.

traveling by plane or boat	the dark	heights
public speaking	going to a new country	elevators
meeting new people	interviewing for a job	highway driving
a specific animal	a specific person	taking tests
bridges	going to the hospital	drowning

A Look at Humberto's Speech Preparation Worksheet. Notice the information and details he provides to help you understand his fear.

Speech Preparation Worksheet: Humberto's Fear

INTRODUCTION

Attention-getting opener

—I *crossed my fingers* [saying] and prayed.
—first time in small plane
—weather very bad
—plane engine stopped

Statement of fear

	This was the beginning of my great fear of flying in small planes.
BODY 1. When and where did the fear develop?	last year, while flying from Cancun to Cozumel
2. What was the situation?	—the weather was very bad —thunder & lightning —rain —pilot couldn't see —plane started to shake —engine stopped
3. Who were you with?	only the pilot
4. How did you feel at the time?	—I began to tremble & sweat —felt like I was in a paper airplane —thought "I'm too young to die"
5. How did the situation end?	—pilot stayed calm —engine started again —"no te preocupes" —we landed safely in Cozumel —celebrated by buying ice cream; It *melted in my mouth* [saying]
6. Have you tried to overcome the fear? How?	—I'll never overcome it

CONCLUSION

—Now you know why I am afraid of small planes.
—Makes me upset
—I'll never fly in a small plane again!
—Thank you.

B Read the instructions for organizing your speech.

Introduction
1. Include an attention-getting opener.
2. Say what your fear is.

Body
Provide details about your fear and how it developed.
1. When/Where did it develop?
2. What was the situation?
3. Who were you with?
4. How did you feel at the time?
5. How did the situation end?
6. How have you tried to overcome your fear?

Conclusion
1. Make a final statement(s) your audience will remember.
2. Thank your audience for listening to you.

C Now complete your own Speech Preparation Worksheet on the next page. You may change some questions or add your own.

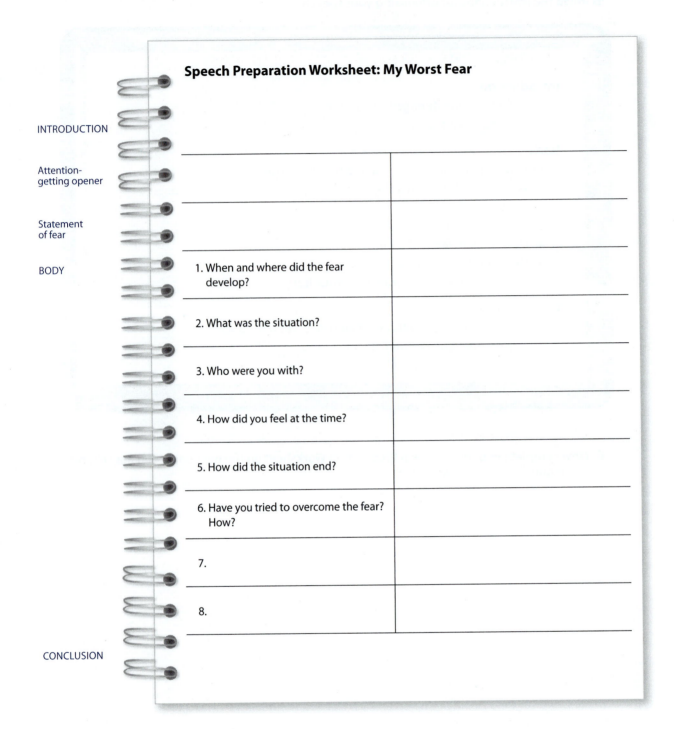

Speech Preparation Worksheet: My Worst Fear

INTRODUCTION

Attention-
getting opener

Statement
of fear

BODY

1. When and where did the fear
   develop?

2. What was the situation?

3. Who were you with?

4. How did you feel at the time?

5. How did the situation end?

6. Have you tried to overcome the fear?
   How?

7.

8.

CONCLUSION

D Read the Useful Language expressions you can use to conclude your speech. Place a checkmark (✓) next to the expressions you like best.

> **USEFUL LANGUAGE: CONCLUDING YOUR SPEECH**
>
> _____ Now you know why I am afraid of . . .
>
> _____ I'm sure you understand why I am so scared of . . .
>
> _____ This explains my terrible fear of . . .
>
> _____ Thank you so much for listening this morning (afternoon).
>
> _____ Other: _____

E Select a saying from pages 34–35 to include in your speech. Write it here:

_____.

F Prepare at least two speech aids. Describe them here:

1 _____

2 _____

STEP 3 | Prepare Note Cards

A Use the instructions in step 2B to prepare note cards for your speech. Label the cards _Introduction, Body,_ and _Conclusion._

B Fill in details from your Speech Preparation Worksheet. Use as many cards as you need.

C Add one of the Useful Language expressions above and a saying from pages 34–35 to your notes.

D Note where you will present your speech aids.

E Number your cards.

STEP 4 | Practice Your Speech

A Practice your speech in front of a mirror using your note cards and speech aids. Record the speech and listen to it at least once. Make sure it is two to three minutes long.

B Complete the Speech Checklist. Is there anything you want to change or improve before you present your speech in class?

Speech Checklist	YES	NO
1. In my introduction I included an attention-getting opener and I stated my fear.	❏	❏
2. I included details about my fear.	❏	❏
3. I prepared a conclusion and thanked the audience for listening.	❏	❏
4. I included two speech aids.	❏	❏
5. I included a saying from the chapter.	❏	❏
6. I included a Useful Language expression.	❏	❏
7. My pronunciation of regular past-tense verbs is correct.	❏	❏
8. My speech is two to three minutes long.	❏	❏

C Practice again with your note cards and speech aids.

D Your teacher and/or your classmates may evaluate your speech. Study the form on page 142 so you know how you will be evaluated. You may use the items on the form to make final changes to your speech.

STEP 5 | Present Your Speech

A Relax, take a deep breath, and present your speech.

B Listen to your audience's applause.

CHAPTER 4

INTERESTING INTERVIEWS

An interview is a conversation between two people. One person asks another person questions to get information. The person who asks the questions is called the *interviewer*. The person who answers the questions is called the *interviewee*.

CHAPTER CHALLENGE: Your challenge in this chapter is to learn how to be a good interviewer. By the time you complete this chapter, you will be able to:

- identify different types of questions used by interviewers
- plan, prepare, and conduct an informal interview
- prepare a speech about the information from the interview

I. Types of Interview Questions

Read about the types of questions you can ask in informal interviews.

Open-ended Questions

These are general information questions. They begin with *wh-* words or *how*. The interviewer does not expect any particular answer. The interviewee may answer in any way he or she likes.

EXAMPLES:
- What is your opinion about the candidates for president?
- Why do you hope Mrs. Kenney wins?

Yes/No Questions

The interviewer expects an answer that starts with "yes" or "no." Following one of these answers, the interviewee may add an explanation.

EXAMPLES:
- Do you think Mrs. Kenney is qualified?
- Will you vote for her?

Directed-Response Questions

These questions ask for specific information. The interviewer expects the interviewee to give this information in the answer.

EXAMPLES:
- Which candidate do you prefer?
- How old were you the first time you voted?

Scale Questions

These are questions that ask the interviewee to rank a subject on a scale.

EXAMPLE:

What grade would you give the president?   Poor   Fair   Average   Good   Excellent

ACTIVITY Identify the Question Type

1 Work with a partner. Analyze the following questions. Write the letter of the correct question type on the line next to each question.

(a) Open-ended   (b) Yes/No   (c) Directed response   (d) Scale

_____ 1. How many years have you been a teacher?

_____ 2. Why did you decide to become a teacher?

_____ 3. What level do you teach?

_____ 4. Where did you get your degree?

_____ 5. Do you enjoy teaching?

_____ 6. What do you dislike about teaching?

_____ 7. On a scale of 1 to 5, how do you like your job?

_____ 8. Has the teaching profession changed in the last five years?

_____ 9. How likely are you to recommend the teaching profession to young people who are still in school? Circle your answer.   Very Likely   Somewhat Likely   Unlikely

_____ 10. What advice would you give to new teachers?

2 **Think of another example of each type of question to use in an interview with a teacher.**

1. Open-ended: _____

2. Yes/No: _____

3. Directed response: _____

4. Scale: _____

3 **Share your questions with the class.**

II. Follow-up Questions

After an interviewee answers a question, you may decide you want more information about the same topic. You can get more information by asking *follow-up questions*. Most follow-up questions begin with *wh-* words or *how*.

EXAMPLE:

Question:	Do you have any brothers or sisters?
Answer:	Yes, I have two brothers.
Follow-up Question:	How old are they?

ACTIVITY **Ask Follow-up Questions**

1 **Work in small groups. Read the interview questions and sample answers. List three follow-up questions you could ask. Include a variety of question types.**

EXAMPLE:

Question:	Do you have any pets?
Answer:	No, I don't.

Follow-up questions:

a. Why not?	(open-ended)
b. Do you like animals?	(yes/no)
c. What kind of pet would you like to have?	(directed response)

1. Question: Have you ever had a job?

    Answer: No, I haven't.

    a. _____

    b. _____

    c. _____

2. Question: Do you like to watch movies?

    Answer: Yes, I love to watch movies.

    a. _____

    b. _____

    c. _____

3. Question: Are you a good cook?

    Answer: No, not really.

    a. _____

    b. _____

    c. _____

4. Question: Do you like to travel?

   Answer: Yes, I take a trip every year.

   a. _____

   b. _____

   c. _____

5. Question: Do you have any hobbies?

   Answer: Yes, I have a few.

   a. _____

   b. _____

   c. _____

2 **Share your follow-up questions with the class.**

3 **Work with a partner. Role-play short conversations using the questions, answers, and follow-up questions you wrote.**

III. The Parts of an Interview

There is more to an interview than just asking questions! Read the guidelines for steps to take before, during, and after the interview.

Before the Interview

1. Choose the person to interview. Set a time and place for the meeting.
2. Prepare a list of questions and possible follow-up questions you want to ask.
3. Organize items you will need such as your computer or a notebook for taking notes. You may also want to record the interview using a voice or video recorder.

During the Interview

1. Before asking your prepared questions, greet your interviewee, ask some casual questions, or give a compliment. This step will help both of you to relax.
   EXAMPLES:
   How are you? What have you been doing lately? Are you still taking tennis lessons? I see you have a new car. It's beautiful.

2. Ask your prepared questions.
3. Ask follow-up questions.
4. Show interest in the speaker. You can do this in two ways.

   a. Use gestures and facial expressions. For example, nod your head, smile, and look directly at the speaker's face.

   b. Use short expressions or exclamations to show your interest.
   EXAMPLES:
   Wow, that's interesting, good, yes, great, that's lucky, how awful, uh-huh

5. Ask your interviewee to repeat or explain an answer if necessary.

   EXAMPLES:

   Wait, I don't understand. I'm sorry, I didn't get that. Could you repeat that?

6. Before concluding, ask if there is anything else the interviewee would like to say. Ask for permission to contact the speaker later if necessary, and thank him or her for the interview.

After the Interview

1. Review your notes as soon as possible while you still remember all the details.
2. Add missing information to your notes.
3. Make sure you can read your own writing.

ACTIVITY   **Practice Interviewing**

Conduct a one- to two-minute practice interview about a trip or a vacation. Work in groups of three. One student will be the interviewer; another will be the interviewee; the third will be an observer. Follow these steps:

1. The interviewer asks the interviewee questions and follow-up questions about a trip or vacation.

2. The observer listens and fills out the checklist below.

3. The observer checks the time and stops the interview after two minutes.

4. Group members discuss the checklist after the interview.

5. Group members then switch roles. Each student should practice each role.

Observer's Checklist

Put a checkmark (✓) next to the verbal and body language the interviewer used. Write additional expressions the interviewer used.

1. Casual Conversation

   ____ *Good morning.*____ *How are you?* ____ *How's it going?* ____ *What's new?*

   ____ A compliment: _____

   ____ Other casual comments or questions: _____

2. Types of Questions

   ____ Open-ended: (Example: _____)

   ____ Yes/No: (Example: _____)

   ____ Directed response: (Example: _____)

   ____ Scale: (Example: _____)

3. Follow-up Questions

   ____ *Who ... ?*   ____ *What ... ?*   ____ *When ... ?*

   ____ *Where ... ?*   ____ *Why ... ?*   ____ *How ... ?*

   Examples: _____

   _____

4. Verbal Encouragement

   ____ *That's interesting.*   ____ *Wow!*   ____ *Yes*

   ____ *Uh huh*   ____ *How awful*   ____ *Great*

   Other: _____

   (continued)

(Continued)

5. Encouraging Body Language

_____ good eye contact   _____ nodding head   _____ smiling

6. Asking for Clarification

_____ *Could you repeat that?*   _____ *I don't understand.*

_____ *I'm sorry. I missed that.*   _____ *Please say that again.*

Other: _____

7. Before Concluding

_____ Invited the interviewee to make any other comments.

_____ Thanked interviewee.

IV. Presentation Preview

Your project in this chapter has two parts. First you will plan and conduct an interview with someone who is not a classmate. Then you will present a speech about the interview in class.

ACTIVITY 1   **Listen to a Model Interview**

Listen to the Model Interview. Pay attention Boris's questions and the way he encourages Jeremy to provide more information.

MODEL INTERVIEW: An Embarrassing Situation

Boris: Hi, Jeremy. *What's new?*

Jeremy: Hey, Boris. I'm fine. *What's up with you?*

Boris: I'm great. Like I told you on the phone, I'm doing a project for school. I'm supposed to interview a friend about a memorable experience. Could you tell me about an unusual or special experience you've had lately?

Jeremy: Sure. I'll tell you about a really embarrassing experience. My pants ripped while I was at work!

Boris: I'm sorry, I missed that. Could you repeat what you said?

Jeremy: My pants. I tore them at work.

Boris: [*Laughing*] Oh no! When?

Jeremy: About a month ago.

Boris: Where do you work?

Jeremy: At a law office.

Boris: What happened exactly?

Jeremy: It was my first day as a lawyer in my law firm. An hour after I arrived, I bent over to pick up a file from the floor and my pants tore.

Boris: That's awful! What did you do?

Jeremy: I called a cab to take me home, but the driver wouldn't take me because I only live three blocks away. He said he wouldn't make enough money. Then he laughed at me and drove away.

Boris: What did you do after that?

Jeremy: I covered my behind with a folder and walked home!

Boris: That's so funny! On a scale of 1 to 10, how embarrassed were you?

Jeremy: Definitely a 10! It was the most embarrassing experience of my life.

* *What have you been doing lately?*

* *How are you?*

Boris:	I bet it was! Before we finish, is there anything else you'd like to say?
Jeremy:	Yes. From now on I will always check my pants before I leave my house.
Boris:	That sounds like a good plan. Thanks for taking the time for this interview, Jeremy. Can I call you if I have any other questions?
Jeremy:	Of course.
Boris:	That's great. Thank you again. See you later.

ACTIVITY 2 **Complete the Questions**

1 **Listen to Boris's interview with Jeremy again. Complete the questions that Boris asked.**

a. Hi, Jeremy. _____?

b. Could you tell me about an _____ or special _____ you've had lately?

c. Could you _____ what you _____?

d. (*One word*) _____ ?

e. Where do you _____?

f. What _____ exactly?

g. That's awful! What did _____?

h. _____ after that?

i. On a scale of 1 to 10, _____?

j. Before we finish, _____ you'd like to say?

k. _____ if I have any other _____?

2 **Work with a partner and compare answers. For each item, identify the question type.**

ACTIVITY 3 **Discuss the Model Interview**

Work in small groups. Discuss the questions.

1. How did Boris encourage Jeremy to describe his situation?
2. What question did Boris ask to start the interview?
3. What kinds of follow-up questions did Boris ask?
4. Did Boris need Jeremy to make something clearer? How do you know?
5. What other questions would you have asked Jeremy?

V. Reporting on an Interview

Your speaking task in this chapter is to prepare a two- to three-minute speech about your interview. You will use your own words to report about your interviewee's answers to your interview questions. You will also use rhetorical questions (described below) to move your speech along and make it lively.

A. Quotations and Restatements

When reporting your interviewee's answers, you can use either direct quotations or restatements of the speaker's words. A *quotation* is a repetition of the speaker's exact words. A *restatement* keeps the speaker's meaning but uses your own words. Study the examples.

Quotation: Jeremy told the driver, "I'll give you a five-dollar tip."
Restatement: Jeremy told the driver he would give him a five-dollar tip. *Or* Jeremy offered to give the driver a five-dollar tip.

Quotation: Carlos told Ahmed, "I think I lost my passport."
Restatement: Carlos told Ahmed he thinks he lost his passport.

Quotation: Maria said, "I hope he finds it!"
Restatement: Maria said she hopes he finds it.

ACTIVITY 1 Practice Making Restatements

1 Work with a partner. Restate the quotations in your own words.

EXAMPLE:

Carlos: "I think I lost my passport."

Restatement: <u>Carlos said he thinks he lost his passport.</u>

a. *Lisa:* "I had no time to study for the spelling test."

Restatement: Lisa said _____

b. *Karen:* "I know I failed the test."

Restatement: Karen thinks _____

c. *Horatio:* "My car wouldn't start, so I was late to class."

Restatement: Horatio explained _____

d. *David:* "Next time your car won't start, call me, and I'll drive you to school."

Restatement: David offered _____

e. *Hans:* "I want to ask my girlfriend to marry me."

Restatement: Hans told me _____

2 Share your restatements with the class.

B. Rhetorical Questions

Rhetorical questions are questions that a speaker asks to make a speech interesting and lively. The speaker does not expect listeners to answer these questions.

EXAMPLE:

My teacher speaks five languages. *Isn't that amazing?*

ACTIVITY 2 **Identify Rhetorical Questions**

Work with a partner. Read the statements and the two questions that follow. One question is rhetorical. The other is a true question. Underline the rhetorical question.

EXAMPLE:

Tim's neighbor won the lottery!

a. <u>Isn't that great?</u>

b. How much did he win?

1. Our friend ran 30 miles.

   a. How long did it take him?

   b. Do you think his feet were tired?

2. My sister went mountain climbing.

   a. Where does she get her energy?

   b. Where did she go?

3. Susa's little brother has lots of accidents. Yesterday, he fell off his bicycle.

   a. What will he do next?

   b. Was he hurt?

4. First they had a flat tire, then their car was stolen.

   a. When did this happen?

   b. Can you believe their bad luck?

5. Jean has been in college for six years.

   a. Will she ever graduate?

   b. Is she a full-time or part-time student?

ACTIVITY 3 **Listen to the Model Speech**

Listen to Boris's Model Speech about his interview with Jeremy. Pay attention to his use of quotations, restatements, and rhetorical questions.

Model Speech: My Interview with Jeremy

INTRODUCTION   Have you ever had a really embarrassing experience? *What comes to mind?*

                My neighbor, Jeremy, is 25 years old. He just graduated from law school and started his first job. He told me he had an embarrassing experience at work, and he let me interview him about it. You won't believe what happened to him!

BODY   It was Jeremy's first day as a lawyer in a law firm. He told me that one hour after he arrived, he bent over to pick up a file from the floor, and guess what happened? The seat of his pants tore open!

* What ideas do you have?

(continued)

(Continued)

What do you think Jeremy did? Well, he called a cab to take him home so he could change his pants. He lives very close to his office—only three blocks away, but the taxi driver wouldn't take him. Can anyone guess why? I'll tell you! The driver said he wouldn't make enough money going only three blocks. He just laughed at Jeremy and drove away. Can you believe that?

So, what do you think Jeremy did next? He covered the tear in his pants with a folder and walked home. I bet he looked something like this.

Jeremy told me this was the most embarrassing experience of his life. Then I asked him if he wanted to say anything else. He told me that from now on, he will always check his pants before he leaves his house!

CONCLUSION   In conclusion, I hope nothing like this ever happens to me—or to any of you!

Thank you so much for listening to this report about my interview with Jeremy.

ACTIVITY 4 **Model Speech Discussion**

  Listen to Boris's speech again. Then work in small groups and discuss the questions.

1. How did Boris start his speech? Was this an effective way to begin?

2. What information did Boris provide about his interviewee?

3. List five rhetorical questions that Boris asked.

   a. _____

   b. _____

   c. _____

   d. _____

   e. _____

4. Did you like the way Boris used rhetorical questions? Why or why not?

5. How did Boris restate Jeremy's answers? Give examples.

6. How did Boris conclude his speech?

VI. Pronunciation Practice: Intonation in Questions

Intonation means the way your voice rises and falls when you speak. Your voice should go up at the end of questions that can be answered with "yes" or "no."

EXAMPLES:

Are you happy? ➚   Is it raining? ➚

Your voice should go down at the end of *Wh-* and *How* questions.

EXAMPLES:

When did you arrive? ➘   Who is your advisor? ➘

ACTIVITY 1 Practice the Intonation of Yes/No Questions

Listen and repeat the *Yes/No* questions. Be sure your voice rises at the end of each question.

1. Can you see?
2. Are you going?
3. Is he here?
4. Do you like this class?
5. Will you stay?
6. May I sit down?
7. Have you had dinner?
8. Would you like some tea?
9. Did you go shopping?
10. Does he know you?

ACTIVITY 2 Practice the Intonation of *Wh-* Questions

Listen and repeat the *Wh-* questions. Be sure your voice falls at the end of each question.

1. Where do you live?
2. When is your birthday?
3. How old are you?
4. Why were you absent?
5. What is your name?
6. Who is your favorite actor?
7. How do you get to school?
8. What time do you wake up?
9. Where do you buy your clothes?
10. Why are you studying English?

ACTIVITY 3 Identify the Correct Intonation

1 Work with a partner. Look back at the questions in Activity 2, page 47. Insert rising and falling arrows to show the intonation of the questions.

EXAMPLES:

Could you repeat what you said? ➚

Where do you work? ➘

2 Practice the Model Interview on page 46 with your partner. Make sure to use correct question intonation.

VII. Playing with Sayings: Sayings in Question Form

ACTIVITY 1 Learn the Meanings

Read the following sayings and their meanings. Place a checkmark (✓) next to the ones you heard in the model interview on page 46 and in Boris's speech on pages 49–50.

_____ 1. **Where's the fire?** Why are you in such a hurry?
Why are you rushing off without saying goodbye? *Where's the fire?*

_____ 2. **Do you read me?** Do you understand me?
I will not allow you to stay out after dark. *Do you read me?*

_____ 3. **What comes to mind?** What ideas do you have?
What comes to mind when you think about your best friend?

_____ 4. **What's new?** What have you been doing lately?
Hi, I haven't seen you for a while! *What's new?*

_____ 5. **What's up (with you)?** How are you? What's new? *or* What's the matter with you?
You are usually so happy; today you are sad. *What's up (with you)?*

1 Work in small groups. Underline the sentence that best shows the meaning of the saying in italics.

1. *What's new?*

    a. What did you get for your birthday?

    b. How have you been spending your time?

    c. Will you show me the new things you bought?

2. *What comes to mind?*

    a. Who will watch the baby?

    b. Why are you so forgetful?

    c. What ideas do you have?

3. *Where's the fire?*

    a. Whose house is on fire?

    b. Why are you in such a big hurry?

    c. Who called the fire department?

4. *What's up with you?*

    a. How was your flight?

    b. Where have you been?

    c. What's the matter with you?

5. *Do you read me?*

    a. Would you like to read a book?

    b. Can you see me clearly?

    c. Were my directions clear to you?

2 Fill in the saying that best completes each sentence.

   a. The teacher asked the class, "_____ when you think of summer?"

   b. When I saw my friend running very fast, I asked him, "_____?"

   c. Gottfried was in a bad mood and I didn't know why. I asked him, "_____?"

   d. My neighbor always greets me by asking, "_____?"

   e. Lisbet's father told her she had to be home by 8:00 pm. To make sure she heard him, he asked her, "_____?"

VIII. Presentation Project: Report on an Interview

Your project is to interview someone about a personal experience and present a speech about the interview.

STEP 1 | Conduct an Interview

A Choose a person to interview. The person you select should not be one of your classmates. It could be, for example,

a friend	a neighbor	a teacher	a relative
your dentist	your doctor	a librarian	a teammate

B Review the information on pages 44–45 about what to do before, during, and after the interview.

STEP 2 | Plan Your Speech

A Reread Boris's Model Speech on pages 49–50.

B Read the guidelines for organizing your speech.

Introduction
1. Get your listeners' attention with your first statement.
2. Briefly describe your interviewee, for example:
   - who the interviewee is and how you know him or her
   - what he or she does
   - how old he or she is

Body
1. Report on the information from the interview in your own words. Include:
   - what happened to your interviewee
   - when and where it happened
   - why or how it happened
   - who was involved
   - what happened in the end
   - how the interviewee reacted
2. Include at least three rhetorical questions to involve your audience.

Conclusion
1. Make a final statement that your audience will remember.
2. Thank your audience for listening.

C Read the Useful Language expressions you can use to change quotations to restatements. Place a checkmark (✓) next to the expressions you like best.

USEFUL LANGUAGE: INTRODUCING RESTATEMENTS

_____ (My teacher) said . . .

_____ Then she said . . .

_____ Jack's friend told him . . .

_____ Jeremy explained that . . .

_____ Cara asked if . . .

_____ Inna offered to . . .

D Include at least one speech aid.

E Select a saying from page 51 to include in your speech. Write it here:

_____

STEP 3 | Prepare Note Cards

A Use the guidelines in Step 2, page 53 to prepare note cards for your speech. Label the cards *Introduction, Body, Conclusion.*

B Fill in details from your interview notes. Use as many cards as you need.

C Add a saying from page 51 to your notes.

D Number your cards.

STEP 4 | Practice Your Speech

A Practice your speech with your note cards. Record it and listen to it at least once. Be sure it is two to three minutes long.

B Complete the Speech Checklist. Is there anything you want to change or improve before you present the speech in class?

Speech Checklist	YES	NO
1. In my introduction I included an attention getter and a description of my interviewee.	☐	☐
2. I included details from the interview.	☐	☐
3. I included restatements of my interviewee's answers.	☐	☐
4. I included at least three rhetorical questions.	☐	☐
5. I included a conclusion and thanked the audience for listening.	☐	☐
6. I included a saying from the chapter.	☐	☐
7. I included a speech aid.	☐	☐
8. My intonation at the end of questions is correct.	☐	☐
9. My speech is two to three minutes long.	☐	☐

C Practice again with your note cards.

D Your teacher and/or your classmates may evaluate your speech. Study the form on page 143 so you know how you will be evaluated. You may use the checklist to make final changes to your speech.

STEP 5 | Present Your Speech

A Relax, take a deep breath, and present your speech.

B Listen to your audience's applause!

CHAPTER 5

EXPLAIN IT!

Speeches can have different purposes. Probably the most common one is to inform or explain something. When you give a speech like this, your job is to be a teacher. You need to present facts—not opinions—to help the audience understand and remember the information you want them to learn.

CHAPTER CHALLENGE Your challenge in this chapter is to learn how to teach your audience about a problem. By the time you complete this chapter, you will be able to:

- identify a problem and explain its causes
- present solutions to the problem
- plan, prepare, and present a speech to inform using a problem-solution organization

I.   Identify a Problem

There are many problems in the world today. Some are specific to a school or community, while others are international problems that affect people all over the world. There are environmental problems as well as social problems. Most people have large or small personal problems as well.

ACTIVITY 1 **Brainstorm Problems**

Work in small groups. Brainstorm problems and add them to the categories in the chart. Examples are provided. Can you think of other problems that don't fit these categories? Add them at the end.

School Problems	International Problems
cheating on tests	world hunger

Community Problems	Environmental Problems
car theft	global warming

National Problems	Health/Psychological Problems
homelessness	stress

Problems Specific to a Country	Other Problems
dengue fever in Brazil	

II. Analyze a Problem

In order to analyze a problem and explain it, you will need to talk about what causes it and how to solve it. Study the examples in the chart.

Problem	Causes	Solutions
Homelessness	-Not enough low-income housing -Job loss	-The government needs to build more low-income housing. -Communities need more job-training programs.
Shark attacks at beach	- Shiny objects attract sharks. - Blood attracts sharks.	-Don't wear jewelry in the water. -Don't enter the water if you are bleeding.
Teen shoplifting	- Items are easy to steal. - It's a "game" for teenagers.	- Stores can attach electronic sensors to merchandise. - Schools should teach teens about the bad effects of stealing.

ACTIVITY Analyze a Problem

1 Work with a partner. Analyze the following facts about the problem of insomnia—being unable to sleep. Label each statement C for cause or S for solution.

_____ a. Suffering from depression

_____ b. Drinking coffee in the late afternoon

_____ c. Staying awake all day without napping

_____ d. Being worried or afraid of something, such as giving a speech

_____ e. Feeling stressed

_____ f. Drinking alcohol or smoking before bedtime

_____ g. Exercising early in the day, not in the evening

_____ h. Having a quiet, dark, and cool bedroom

_____ i. Listening to soft music at bedtime

2 Brainstorm with your partner. What other causes and solutions for insomnia can you think of?

3 Share your ideas with the class.

III. Parts of a Speech

In Chapter 1 you learned that every speech has an introduction, a body, a conclusion, and transitions. This section provides additional information about the contents of the introduction, transitions, and conclusion.

A. Introduction

A good introduction contains two parts: an "attention getter" and a preview.

Attention Getter

The purpose of the attention getter is to grab your listeners' attention and motivate them to listen to the rest of your speech.

> **EXAMPLE:**
> Today I am going to give you some information that could save your life!

Preview

The preview comes after the attention-getting opener. It tells your listeners what you are going to speak about. It lets them know what the main points in the body of your speech are going to be.

EXAMPLES:

Today, I will talk about the problem of shark attacks.

First, I will explain why sharks attack swimmers at the beach.

Second, I will tell you how to prevent being attacked by a shark.

B. Transitions

How would you feel if you were driving on a highway and there were no signs? You would feel lost and confused! You wouldn't know where you are or how to get to your destination.

Transitions in your speech are like signs along a highway. They are words and phrases that tell your listeners where you have been and where you are going in your speech.

You will use two types of transitions in this chapter.

Transition to the Body of the Speech

This transition tells listeners that the introduction is over and you are starting the body of your speech.

EXAMPLES:

First, let's look at . . .

To start, I will discuss . . .

To begin, I want to explain . . .

Transitions in the Body of the Speech

These transitions signal that you have finished one section of your speech and are ready to begin the next section. A good way to do this is to review the information you just explained and to preview what you are going to discuss next.

EXAMPLES:

First I explained . . . Second I will talk about . . .

I just talked about. . . . Now I will move on to . . .

Now you know . . . Next, I am going to discuss . . .

C. Conclusion

Summary

Your conclusion should have two parts: a summary and final remarks. The summary reminds your listeners of what you spoke about. It repeats the main points you talked about in the body of your speech.

EXAMPLES:

Today, I talked about the problem of shark attacks.

First, I explained why sharks attack swimmers at the beach.

After that I told you how to prevent being attacked by a shark.

Final Remarks

Your final remarks should end your speech smoothly and memorably.

EXAMPLE:

Now that you know how to stay safe from sharks, grab your sunglasses and bathing suits and let's go to the beach!

Work with a partner. Pretend that you are giving a speech about insomnia. Read the Speech Preparation Outline below and fill in each blank line with the correct statement from the list.

1. Now you know what causes insomnia. Next, I'd like to explain what you can do about it.
2. After that, I will explain some solutions to this annoying problem.
3. To start with, let's talk about the reasons people have insomnia.
4. Second, I discussed solutions to the problem of insomnia.
5. First, I will explain some causes of insomnia.

Introduction

Attention Getter

I love to sleep! I would be miserable if I didn't get a good night's sleep. Unfortunately millions of people have trouble falling asleep at night. They suffer from a very common problem.

Statement and Explanation of Problem

It's called *insomnia*. Insomnia is the inability to fall asleep or to stay asleep.

Preview

Today, I will explain the problem of insomnia.

_____

_____

Transition to Body:

_____

Body

I. Reasons for Insomnia

    A. Drinking coffee in the late afternoon
    B. Stress or anxiety about personal problems
    C. Drinking alcohol before bedtime

Transition:

_____

II. Solutions to Insomnia.

    A. Make sure your bedroom is dark and quiet.
    B. Avoid smoking before bedtime.
    C. Don't exercise within 3 hours of bedtime.

(continued)

(Continued)

Conclusion

Summary

I have explained two important aspects about insomnia.

First, I talked about causes of insomnia.

_____.

Final Remark(s)

So, follow the advice I have given you and you will get a good night's sleep tonight!

IV. Presentation Preview

Your goal is to choose a problem you feel strongly about and to prepare a speech to inform your audience about it.

 ACTIVITY 1 **Listen to a Model Speech**

Listen to Igor's model speech. Pay attention to the parts of the speech and the details Igor includes.

Model Speech: Stage Fright

INTRODUCTION

Attention Getter

What do you have in common with famous athletes, actors, singers, and even presidents? It's a common problem that causes pain and suffering. Can you guess what it is? I'll tell you.

Igor showed this illustration.

Statement and Explanation of Problem

It's called stage fright!

Stage fright is the fear you have when you speak or perform in front of an audience. It makes you feel like you *have butterflies in your stomach!*

Preview

Today, I will teach you two important points about stage fright. First, I'll explain the causes of stage fright. Second, I'll tell you some ways you can control it.

Transition to Body

Let's begin by looking at the causes.

BODY

I looked up *stage fright* in Wikipedia. I read that unfamiliar activities create stress and cause stage fright. The article also said that people get stage fright when they feel they are not prepared. I know I get it if I haven't practiced my speech at least three times!

* Feel very nervous!

Wikipedia says there are other causes of stage fright, too. Some people lack confidence about their language skills. Some people are afraid to fail. They are afraid they will forget what they want to say or that the audience won't like them. These feelings can all cause stage fright.

Transition Now you know some of the causes of stage fright. Next I will explain what you can do about it.

There are several solutions to the problem. Wear something you feel good in! I know I don't feel as nervous when I look my best. It also helps to practice deep breathing before your speech. This helps you to feel calm. Start your speech slowly. Take time to arrange your note cards and make eye contact with the audience before beginning. This will help you relax. Another great suggestion offered by experts is to pretend that you are talking to friends. Thinking of my audience as good friends really works for me.

Finally, it is very important to be prepared. So practice your speech many times. This will help you feel more confident. I can tell you from personal experience that being prepared really reduces my stage fright.

CONCLUSION
Summary I have explained two important aspects of stage fright. First, I explained the different causes of stage fright. Second, I talked about ways to help you control it.

Final Remarks In conclusion, stage fright does not have to be your *worst nightmare.* Remember, as long as you are in control of it, your stage fright won't be *a roadblock.* Stage fright is like a lion in a cage. If you don't let it out of the cage, it can't harm you!

* *The most terrible thing that can happen*

* *Serious difficulty*

ACTIVITY 2 **Complete the Outline**

1 **Listen to Igor's speech again and complete the outline on page 62.**

Introduction
Attention Getter

What do you have in common with _____ athletes, actors, singers, and even _____? It's a _____ problem that causes _____ and suffering. Can you _____ what it is? I'll tell you.

Statement and Explanation of Problem

It's called _____. Stage fright is the _____ you have when you speak or perform in front of an _____.

Preview

Today, I will _____ you two important points about _____.

    A. Causes of stage fright

    B. _____

Transition to Body

Let's begin by looking at _____.

Body

I. Causes of stage fright.

    A. Causes according to Wikipedia

        1. Unfamiliar activities

        2. Feeling you are _____

        3. Lack of _____

        4. Fear of failure _____

           a. fear of forgetting _____

           b. _____

Transition

Now you know some of the causes of stage fright. _____ I will explain what you can do about it.

II. Solutions for stage fright

    A. _____

    B. Practice deep breathing before speech

    C. _____

    D. Arrange your cards and _____

    E. Pretend you are talking with friends

    F. Be prepared. _____ your speech many times.

Conclusion

Summary

I have explained two important aspects of stage fright.

    A. First, I explained the different causes of stage fright.

    B. Second, I talked about_____.

Final Remarks

In conclusion, stage fright does not have to be your worst _____.
Remember, as long as you are in control of it, your stage fright won't be a
roadblock. Stage fright is like a _____ in a cage. If you don't let it
out of the _____, it can't harm you!

2 Work with a partner. Compare your completed outlines.

ACTIVITY 3 **Model Speech Discussion**

Discuss these questions in small groups.

1. Was "stage fright" a good topic for Igor's speech? Why?

2. How did Igor use his personal experiences to develop the body of his speech?

3. Where did Igor use transitions?

4. Was Igor's information well organized? Why or why not?

5. How did you know when he was beginning his summary?

6. How does Igor's summary differ from his preview?

7. What do you remember most about his speech?

V. Pronunciation Practice: Syllable Stress in Compound Nouns

A compound noun is formed by combining two nouns into one word or phrase. Some compound
nouns are written as single words, like *chalkboard* or *classroom*. Others are written as two words, like *stop
sign*, *note card*, and *eye contact*. When pronouncing compound nouns, stress the first syllable or word.

ACTIVITY 1 **Word Practice**

Listen and repeat the following compound nouns. Be sure to stress the first word or syllable
in each item.

1. suntan	5. baseball	9. grapefruit	13. dollhouse	17. mailman
2. football	6. keyhole	10. blueberry	14. swimsuit	18. mailbox
3. airplane	7. suitcase	11. bedroom	15. forehead	19. post office
4. ice cream	8. drugstore	12. bookstore	16. notebook	20. race horse

ACTIVITY 2 **Sentence Practice**

Work with a partner. Write five sentences using at least two of the compound nouns from
Activity 1 in each sentence. Practice reading your sentences aloud to each other.

EXAMPLE: My sister has a **doll**house in her **bed**room.
           The **base**ball hit me on the **fore**head.

1. _____

2. _____

3. _____

4. _____

5. _____

1 Igor's Model Speech on pages 60–61 uses six compound nouns. Three are written as one word. Three are written as two words. Find the compounds and write them in the chart.

One-Word Compound Nouns	Two-Word Compound Nouns

2 Work with a partner. Take turns using these words in sentences.

3 Change partners. Take turns reading Igor's speech to each other. Pay attention to your pronunciation of compound nouns.

VI. Playing with Sayings: Sayings with Compound Nouns

ACTIVITY 1 **Learn the Meanings**

1 Read the following sayings and their meanings. Place a checkmark (✓) next to those you heard in the Model Speech on pages 60–61.

_____ 1. **Butterflies in one's stomach:** a feeling of nervousness
I get *butterflies in my stomach* when I go on a job interview.

_____ 2. **Like a deer in headlights:** unable to move because of fear
I felt *like a deer in headlights* when I had to give my first speech.

_____ 3. **In a heartbeat:** with no preparation
I would go to Paris *in a heartbeat*.

_____ 4. **One's worst nightmare:** the worst thing that can happen
My worst nightmare is getting into a car accident.

_____ 5. **Hit a roadblock:** to meet serious difficulty or trouble
I *hit a roadblock* while I was writing my term paper, so I went for a walk.

2 Circle all the compound nouns in the sayings in Activity 1. Say them out loud several times. Remember to stress the first word or syllable.

ACTIVITY 2 **Use the Sayings**

1 Complete the sentences with your ideas or experiences.

EXAMPLE: <u>Losing my passport in a foreign country</u> is my worst nightmare.

1. I had butterflies in my stomach when _____.

2. I felt like a deer in the headlights when _____.

3. _____ is my worst nightmare.

4. I would _____ in a heartbeat.

5. I hit a roadblock while I was _____.

2 Work in small groups. Share the sentences you wrote. Be sure to stress the first word or syllable of compound nouns.

VII. Presentation Project: Explain It!

Select a problem that you find interesting. Your project is to prepare and present a three- to four-minute speech about the problem. Your goal is to explain its causes and suggest solutions.

STEP 1 | Choose a Topic

A For your Explain It! speech you can choose a problem from Activity 1: Brainstorm Problems on page 56, a problem from the list below, or another problem you choose.

medical mistakes	noisy neighbors	oversleeping
gossip	gaining weight	talking on a cell phone or texting while
barking dogs	Internet addiction	driving
animal cruelty	cell phone addiction	pronunciation difficulties in English
drunk driving	spending too much money	

B Write the problem you selected here: _____

STEP 2 | Plan Your Speech

A Review your completed outline of Igor's Model Speech on pages 60–61. Pay attention to the parts of the speech.

B Read the guidelines for organizing your speech.

Introduction
1. Get your listeners' attention.
2. State the problem and explain it briefly.
3. Preview the main sections in the body of your speech.
4. Add a transition to the body.

Body
1. Explain the causes of the problem.
2. Add a transition.
3. Present solutions to the problem.

Conclusion
1. Summarize the main sections of your speech.
2. Make final remarks your audience will remember.

C Read the Useful Language feature to learn phrases you can use in your preview statement. Place a checkmark (✓) next to the expressions you like best.

USEFUL LANGUAGE: PREVIEW STATEMENTS

_____ This morning, I will explain two major points about _____.

First I will . . .   Next I will . . .

_____ Today, I will talk to you about the problem of _____.

To begin . . .   Second . . .

_____ The purpose of my speech is to discuss _____.

To start, I will . . .   After that, I will . . .

D Complete the outline for your speech.

Explain It! Speech Preparation Outline

Problem: _____

Introduction
Attention Getter

_____

_____

Statement of Problem and Explanation

_____

_____

Preview

_____

First: _____

Second: _____

Transition to body: _____

_____

Body
Causes

_____

_____

_____

Transition: _____

_____

Solutions

_____

_____

_____

Conclusion

Summary

_____

First: _____

Second: _____

Final Remarks

_____

_____

E Read the Useful Language expressions you can use to begin your summary. Place a checkmark (✓) next to the expressions you like best.

> **USEFUL LANGUAGE: SUMMARY STATEMENTS**
>
> This morning, I explained two points about _____.
>
> In my speech today, I spoke about _____.
>
> Now you understand the problem of _____.
>
> First, I explained the causes of . . . Second, I presented solutions . . .

F Prepare at least one speech aid.

G Select a saying from page 64 to include in your speech. Write it here:

_____.

STEP 3 | Prepare Note Cards

A Use the guidelines in Step 2B, page 65, to prepare note cards for your speech. Label the cards:

- Attention Getter
- Statement and Explanation of Problem
- Preview
- Transition to Body
- Causes of Problem
- Transition to Solutions
- Possible Solutions
- Summary
- Final Remarks

B Fill in details from your Speech Preparation Outline. Use as many cards as you need.

C Add Useful Language expressions from page 67 and a saying from page 64 to your notes.

D Number your cards.

STEP 4 | Practice Your Speech

A Practice your speech with your note cards and speech aid. Record it and listen to it at least once. Be sure it is three to four minutes long.

B Complete the Speech Checklist. Is there anything you want to change or improve before you present the speech in class?

Speech Checklist	YES	NO
1. My introduction included an attention getter, statement and explanation of the problem, and preview.	❏	❏
2. I included information about causes and solutions.	❏	❏
3. I included transitions.	❏	❏
4. My conclusion included a summary and final remarks.	❏	❏
5. I included a saying from the chapter.	❏	❏
6. I included a speech aid.	❏	❏
7. I included a Useful Language expression.	❏	❏
8. My pronunciation of compound nouns is correct.	❏	❏
9. My speech is three to four minutes long.	❏	❏

C Practice again with your note cards and speech aid.

D Your teacher and/or your classmates may evaluate your speech. Study the form on page 144 so you know how you will be evaluated. You may use the items on the form to make final changes to your speech.

STEP 5 | Present Your Speech

A Relax, take a deep breath, and present your speech.

B Listen to your audience's applause.

CHAPTER 6

DEMONSTRATE IT!

Demonstrations, or "how-to speeches," are very popular. Chefs on television demonstrate how to prepare a ten-minute meal. Dancers demonstrate dance steps. Flight attendants on airplanes demonstrate how to put on an oxygen mask. The ability to demonstrate a process so that others can perform it is an art. This chapter will help you master that art!

CHAPTER CHALLENGE Your challenge in this chapter is to teach the audience how to do or make something. By the time you complete this chapter, you will be able to:

- identify a process you can teach to others
- plan, prepare, and present a "how-to" speech with step-by-step organization

I. Demonstration Speeches

Demonstration speeches teach listeners how to do or make something by following a series of steps. At one time or another, most people have the opportunity to demonstrate a skill at work, at school, or at home.

ACTIVITY 1 | Brainstorm People Who Demonstrate Skills

1 Work in small groups. Think of five people who demonstrate something as part of their jobs, hobbies, or volunteer work.

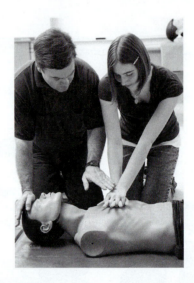

EXAMPLE:
First-aid teachers demonstrate CPR (cardio-pulmonary resuscitation)

1. _____

2. _____

3. _____

4. _____

5. _____

2 Share your answers with the class. Discuss these questions:

  a. Have you seen any of the demonstrations on your list?

  b. Were the demonstrations effective? Why or why not?

ACTIVITY 2 | Identify Topics

1 Work with a partner. Develop a list of possible topics for your own how-to speech.

EXAMPLE:
How to perform basic karate moves
How to create an origami frog

  a. _____

  b. _____

  c. _____

  d. _____

  e. _____

2 Share your topics in small groups. Discuss whether or not you can demonstrate each topic completely in a three- to- four-minute speech.

ACTIVITY 3 **Encourage Audience Participation**

In a how-to speech, it is very effective to give listeners an opportunity to participate. For three of the topics you listed in Activity 2, explain how you could involve the audience.

EXAMPLES:

Topic: How to perform basic karate moves

Audience participation: Ask the audience to stand and perform the karate moves as you demonstrate them.

Topic: How to create an origami frog

Audience participation: Have listeners fold their own pieces of origami paper according to your instructions.

1. _____
2. _____
3. _____

II. Presentation Preview

Your goal in this chapter is to teach your listeners how to do or make something. Your speech will follow a step-by-step organization. By the end of your speech, your listeners will have a new skill.

ACTIVITY 1 **Listen to a Model Speech**

🎧 Listen to Liam's speech about a card trick. Look at the pictures as you listen.

Model Speech: Easy Pick Card Trick

INTRODUCTION Attention Getter	How can you cheer up a friend who is *under the weather*? What's a good way to entertain friends at a party? Why not show them a card trick! Don't worry if you don't know any. I am going to teach you a great one!
Statement of Topic	This morning I will teach you to perform a card trick called "Easy Pick."
Preview	First, I will perform the trick. Then I will teach you how to do it, step by step.
Transition to Body	And now for the trick!
BODY	First, I need a volunteer. Thank you, Lola. Now Lola, pick any card in the deck and remember it.

* Feeling sick

(continued)

(Continued)

And now put your card face down on top of the deck. That's perfect, Lola!

Next, I will put the deck behind my back for a few seconds.

And now, I will show Lola the deck, so she can see the bottom card.

Fourth, I will put the deck behind my back again.

Fifth, I will give the deck to Lola and ask her to shuffle the cards.

And finally, I will look through the deck and find Lola's card.

The three of spades is your card! Thank you for your help, Lola.

Transition Now that you have seen me perform the trick, I will teach it to you step by step.

Step-by-Step Instructions First, ask a friend to pick a card, memorize it, and place it face down on top of the deck, like this.

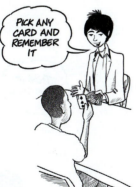

Second, put the deck behind your back and turn over the top card so it faces up.

(continued)

(Continued)

Third, put the deck in front of you so that the bottom card faces your friend and the top card faces you. This is important. Make sure you get a look at that top card.

I'm sure you have just *put two and two together*, and you see that you now know your friend's card!

* *Figured it out*

OK, fourth, this is where it gets a little tricky. Put the deck behind your back again. Turn over the top card—which we already know is the three of spades—and place it back in the deck.

Fifth, ask your friend to shuffle the cards.

Remember, you already know your friend's card. But your friend doesn't know that you already know it!

Finally, look through the deck and find the card. Hand it to your friend and say, "THIS is your card!"

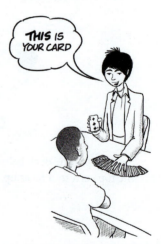

CONCLUSION
Encourage Audience

I hope you have enjoyed learning this trick. If it doesn't work at first, don't *throw in the towel!* Practice the trick a few more times. You will soon perform it perfectly.

* *Don't give up*

Final Remarks

Now go show this trick to your friends and family. I promise you will be *the life of the party!*

* *Funny, outgoing person*

1   **Listen to Liam's Model Speech on pages 71–74 again and complete his note cards.**

1

ATTENTION GETTER

How can you cheer up a friend who is
_____ ?
What's a good way to _____ friends at a
_____ ?
Why not _____ them a _____ trick!
Don't worry if you don't know any.
I am going to _____ you a _____ one!

2

TOPIC

This _____ , I will teach you
to _____ a card trick called
" _____ ."

3

PREVIEW

First, I will _____ the trick.
Then I will _____ you how to _____
it step by _____ .

4

TRANSITION TO BODY

And _____ for the _____ !

5

BODY

First, ask a volunteer to:
  1. _____
  2. remember it _____
  3. place it _____

6

Next, I will put _____ .
    And now,
Lola the deck.
    Fourth, I will _____
again.
    Fifth, I will ask Lola _____ .
    Finally, I will _____
and _____ .

7

TRANSITION

Now that you have seen me perform the trick,
I will _____ it to you _____
by _____.

8

STEP-BY-STEP INSTRUCTIONS

First, ask a friend to:
   1. _____
   2. memorize it
   3. _____.

9

Second, put the deck _____
and turn over the top card so _____
_____.

Third, put the deck in front of you so that:
   1. the bottom card _____
   2. (this is important) the top card _____

10

Fourth, this is where it gets a little tricky.
   1. _____
   2. place it back _____

11

Fifth, _____.
Finally,
   1. _____
   2. Hand it to your friend and say, _____
_____

12

TRANSITION

I hope you _____

13

ENCOURAGING REMARKS

If it doesn't _____ , don't
_____ .
Practice _____ .
You will soon _____ the _____
perfectly!

14

FINAL REMARKS

Now go show this _____ to your
_____ .
I _____ you will be the _____
_____ !

2 Work with a partner. Compare your completed note cards.

ACTIVITY 3 **Perform the Card Trick**

Bring a deck of cards to class. Work in small groups. Read Liam's speech again. Pay attention to the art showing the card trick. Take turns practicing the Easy Pick trick. If you forget a step, review Liam's instructions in his model speech.

ACTIVITY 4 **Model Speech Discussion**

Discuss these questions in small groups.

1. Was teaching a card trick a good topic for this speech? Why or why not?
2. Did Liam have a good attention getter? Why or why not?
3. What were the two main sections in the body of Liam's speech? How did Liam preview each main section?
4. How did Liam emphasize that he was going explain a difficult step?
5. Where did he use transitions?
6. How did he encourage his audience?
7. What were Liam's final remarks?
8. Will you be able to perform this trick in the future? Why or why not?

III. Pronunciation Practice: [θ] and [ð]

English is one of the few languages that has the sounds [θ] (voiceless *th* as in *three*) and [ð] (voiced *th* as in *the*). A common error is to pronounce [t] instead of [θ] and d instead of [ð]. If you do this, *three* sounds like *tree* and *they* sounds like *day*.

To pronounce [θ] and [ð] , place your tongue between your teeth and gently blow out air.

> **PRONUNCIATION TIP**
>
> The letters *th* followed by *e* are usually pronounced [ð].
>
> **Examples**: the   them   other
> bathe   breathe

Contrast Words with [θ] and [ð]

Listen and repeat the following words. Be sure you feel the tip of your tongue between your teeth as you say [θ] and [ð].

[θ]	[ð]
1. thin	6. these
2. thing	7. them
3. think	8. those
4. bath	9. smooth
5. healthy	10. mother

ACTIVITY 2 **Contrast Phrases and Sentences with [θ] and [ð]**

Listen and repeat the phrases and sentences.

[θ]

Phrases	**Sentences**
1. Thanksgiving	Thanksgiving falls on Thursday.
2. thirty-third birthday	Thelma had her thirty-third birthday.
3. something for nothing	You can't get something for nothing.
4. thought-provoking	The author's theme is thought-provoking.
5. back and forth	Beth walked back and forth on the path.

[ð]

6. get together	Let's get together another day.
7. than the other	This is better than the other.
8. smooth leather	My father has a smooth leather belt.
9. either one of them	I'd be happy with either one of them.
10. mother and father	This is my mother and father.

ACTIVITY 3 **Practice the Model Speech**

1 Listen again to the model speech on pages 71–74. Circle the words pronounced with [θ] and underline the words with [ð].

2 Complete the chart with words from Liam's speech.

[θ] (voiceless *th*)		
At the Beginning of Words	**In the Middle of Words**	**At the End of Words**

[ð] (voiced *th*)		
At the Beginning of Words	**In the Middle of Words**	**At the End of Words**

3 Work with a partner. Take turns pronouncing the words aloud several times.

4 Work with a partner. Take turns reading Liam's speech aloud. Be sure you feel your tongue between your teeth as you say [θ] and [ð].

IV. Playing with Sayings: Sayings with [θ] and [ð]

ACTIVITY 1 Learn the Meaning

1 Read the following sayings. Place a checkmark (✓) next to the ones you heard in the Model Speech on pages 71–74.

_____ 1. **The life of the party:** a funny, talkative, outgoing person
Martina is always *the life of the party* because she tells funny jokes.

_____ 2. **Throw in the towel:** to give up
Don't *throw in the towel*; finish your education.

_____ 3. **Put two and two together:** to figure something out; to guess the meaning of something
When we got home and found the door wide open, we put *two and two together*: We'd been robbed!

_____ 4. **Through thick and thin:** in bad times and good times
My best friend has always been there for me *through thick and thin*.

_____ 5. **Be under the weather:** to feel ill
Randy isn't going to the party; he's feeling *under the weather*.

2 Circle the [θ] sounds in the sayings in Activity 1. Underline the [ð] sounds. Then pronounce each saying out loud several times.

ACTIVITY 2 Use the Sayings

1 Work in small groups. Substitute one of the sayings for the italicized words in each sentence. Be sure to use the correct grammatical form of each saying.

1. Helga *gave up* and stopped taking piano lessons.

_____

2. Bill is *feeling sick;* he has a bad cold.

_____

3. The detective collected several clues which helped him *figure out the mystery*.

_____

4. Everyone loves to be friends with Jim because he is always *so entertaining*.

_____

5. Loving families are always there to help one another *when times are hard*.

_____

Take turns reading the sentences aloud to each other. Be sure to pronounce the words [θ] and [ð] correctly.

V. Presentation Project: Demonstrate It!

Your project is to prepare and present a three- to four-minute speech to teach the audience how to do or make something.

STEP 1 | Choose a Topic

1 **You can choose one of the topics from Activity 2: Identify Topics on page 70, one of the topics below, or another topic that interests you. Be sure that you can demonstrate the skill you choose in three to four minutes.**

How to . . .

identify poisonous snakes	teach a dog a trick
give a massage	put air in a tire
make a favorite food	floss your teeth properly
perform a magic trick	teach a parrot to talk
remove ink stains from fabric	identify poison ivy
make a book cover	make a kite
perform a dance	

2 **Write the topic you selected here:** _____ .

STEP 2 | Plan Your Speech

A **Read the guidelines for organizing your speech.**

Introduction
1. Get listeners' attention by asking questions or making a startling statement.
2. State your topic.
3. Preview the body of your speech.

Body
1. Include at least two main sections.
2. Provide step-by-step directions.
3. Emphasize difficult steps.
4. Include transitions.

Conclusion
1. Encourage the audience to learn the new skill.
2. Make final remarks your audience will remember.

B Read the Useful Language expressions you can use to state your speech topic and to preview the main sections in the body. Place a checkmark (✓) next to the expressions you like best.

> **USEFUL LANGUAGE: STATING YOUR TOPIC**
>
> _____ Today I will show you how to . . .
>
> _____ My purpose this morning is to demonstrate . . .
>
> _____ In my speech today, I will teach you how to . . .

> **USEFUL LANGUAGE: PREVIEWING THE BODY OF THE SPEECH**
>
> _____ First, I will show you how to . . .
>
> _____ The first thing I will teach you is . . .
>
> _____ Second, I will demonstrate how . . .
>
> _____ In the last part of my speech, I will . . .

C Complete the outline for your speech.

Demonstrate It! Speech Preparation Outline

Topic: _____

Introduction

Attention Getter

_____

Statement of Topic

_____

Preview

First _____

Second _____

(Third) _____

(Fourth/Finally) _____

Transition

_____

(continued)

(Continued)

Body

First _____

Second _____

(Third) _____

(Fourth/Finally) _____

Speech Aids or Audience Participation

_____

Conclusion

Encouraging remarks

_____

Final Remarks

_____

D Read the Useful Language expressions you can use to signal each step and emphasize difficult steps. Place a checkmark (✓) next to the expressions you like best.

USEFUL LANGUAGE: SIGNALING THE STEPS

_____ First, you need to . . .

_____ The first thing you should do is . . .

_____ Second [Next/ Now], you need to . . .

_____ And for the final step, you need to . . .

_____ The last thing you should do is . . .

USEFUL LANGUAGE: EMPHASIZING DIFFICULT STEPS

_____ The next step is really important.

_____ Listen carefully because step (4) is the hardest of all.

_____ Now pay attention because this step is tricky.

E Select a saying from page 79 to include in your speech. Write it here: _____

F Include one or more speech aids.

STEP 3 | Prepare Note Cards

A Use your Speech Preparation Outline to prepare note cards for your speech. Label the cards

- Attention Getter
- Topic
- Preview

- Transition to body
- Body
- Encourage audience
- Final remarks

B Fill in details from your outline. Use as many cards as you need.

C Write the Useful Language and the saying you selected on your note cards.

D Number your cards.

STEP 4 | Practice Your Speech

A Practice your speech with your note cards and speech aid(s). Record it and listen to it at least once. Make sure it is three to four minutes long.

B Complete the Speech Checklist. Is there anything you want to change or improve before you present the speech in class?

Speech Checklist	YES	NO
1. My introduction included an attention getter, statement of my topic, and a preview.	☐	☐
2. I included all necessary steps in the body of my speech.	☐	☐
3. I included transitions.	☐	☐
4. My conclusion includes listener encouragement and final remarks.	☐	☐
5. I included a saying from the chapter.	☐	☐
6. I included speech aids.	☐	☐
7. I included a Useful Language expression.	☐	☐
8. My pronunciation of [θ] and [ð] is correct.	☐	☐
9. My speech is three to four minutes long.	☐	☐

C Your teacher and/or your classmates may evaluate your speech. Study the form on page 145 so you know how you will be evaluated. You may use the items on the form to make final changes to your speech.

STEP 5 | Present Your Speech

A Relax, take a deep breath, and present your speech.

B Listen to your audience's applause.

CHAPTER 7

COMMUNICATING ACROSS CULTURES

Cross-cultural communication happens whenever we share ideas, thoughts, and **feelings** with people from different cultures. We may do this through speaking, writing, or gesturing. In order to have good, clear communication with people who have different customs and behaviors, we have to learn how to understand the **differences among people** of various cultures.

CHAPTER CHALLENGE Your challenge in this chapter is to understand and enjoy the cultural differences among people. This will help you to communicate with people from all over the world. By the time you complete this chapter, you will be able to:

- appreciate different customs and cultural beliefs
- identify direct and indirect styles of communication
- plan, prepare, and organize a "culture conflict" speech

I. What Is Culture?

Culture consists of the beliefs, values, and behaviors that large groups of people have in common. We learn our culture from our parents, family, friends, and other people we meet and observe all through our lives. One culture is not better than another; each culture is unique!

ACTIVITY 1 Describe Customs

1 Think of a custom that is common in your culture. Choose from one of the following contexts.

giving or receiving gifts	punishing a misbehaving child
the arrival of a new baby	becoming engaged
weddings	dating
funerals	matchmaking
holiday traditions	saying yes or no to an invitation
mealtimes	saying good-bye
greetings	

2 Work in small groups. Explain your custom or tradition to the group.

3 Discuss the following questions.

   a. How did you react when a classmate from another culture described a unique custom?

   b. How did your classmates react to the custom you described?

   c. Which customs from your culture are similar to the ones your classmates described? How?

   d. Which customs from your culture are totally different from the customs that your classmates described? In what way?

ACTIVITY 2 Identify Cultural Beliefs

1 What is true about groups of people in your culture? Complete the statements.

   EXAMPLES:

   Married women _do not travel without their husbands._

   Neighbors _never come to your house without calling first._

   a. Married men _____.

   b. Married women _____.

   c. Young children _____.

   d. Fathers _____.

   e. Mothers _____.

   f. Grandparents _____.

   g. Single men _____.

   h. Single women _____.

   i. Teachers _____.

   j. Students _____.

2 Compare your responses in small groups. Discuss the following questions.

a. Which of your responses were similar to the responses of other group members?

b. Which of your responses were different?

c. Did any of your classmates' responses surprise you? Why?

II. Direct and Indirect Communication Styles

In some cultures, people are very direct. They usually tell others exactly how they think or feel about a situation. People from the United States, Canada, Australia, England, Israel, and Germany tend to communicate very directly. In contrast, people from countries like Japan, China, Korea, Thailand, and Mexico often communicate indirectly. They worry about hurting people's feelings if they disagree or show they are unhappy about a situation. They often avoid direct eye contact with their listeners.

ACTIVITY 1 **Role-play Direct and Indirect Communication Styles**

1 Work with a partner. Choose one of the following situations to role-play.

a. You want to get to know a classmate. You would like to invite him or her for a cup of coffee after class.

b. You have been working for the same company for two years for the same salary. You work very hard. You would like to ask your boss to give you a raise.

c. Your friend borrowed a book from you and hasn't given it back. You need the book to study. You would like your friend to return your book.

d. You just got married. You are shopping for furniture with your spouse. You think the furniture your spouse likes is ugly. You would like to buy different furniture.

e. Your teacher made a mistake grading your exam. She gave you a B instead of a B+. You would like her to correct her mistake.

f. You just had a wonderful lunch in a café with your boyfriend or girlfriend. The waiter brings your bill and has charged you too much for your lunch. You would like the waiter to correct the mistake before you pay.

2 Write a simple dialog about the situation you chose. Think of the words and body language you might use if you have an *indirect* communication style.

EXAMPLE:

Situation: You bought a new portable radio that didn't work properly. You bring it back to the store and show it to the salesman who sold it to you. Your conversation goes like this:

You: I am so sorry to bother you.

Salesman: How can I help you?

You: [*looking down at the floor*] I just bought this radio and it doesn't work.

Salesman: Oh, that's too bad.

You: Isn't there something you can do about this? [*still looking down at the floor*]

Salesman: No, I'm sorry.

You: Thank you anyway. [*You leave the store with the broken radio.*]

3 Now write a dialog about the situation in which you use a *direct* communication style.

EXAMPLE:

You: [*looking directly at the salesman*] Excuse me. I just bought this radio and it doesn't work.

Salesman: Oh, that's too bad.

You: [*still looking directly at the salesman*] I would like a refund, please.

Salesman: I'm sorry, we don't give refunds.

You:	Then I would like to speak to the manager, please. Would you call him?
Manager:	What seems to be the problem here?
You:	I just bought this radio and it doesn't work. Here is my receipt. I would like a refund, please.
Manager:	Of course, I will take care of this for you.
You:	Thank you very much.

4 Act out (role-play) your situation in front of the class twice. First use the indirect communication style. Then use the direct one.

5 After all the role plays, discuss the following questions in small groups:

a. Which communication style are you more comfortable with—direct or indirect?

b. Which style is used most often in your culture?

c. How would people from your culture handle the situations in Activity 1?

ACTIVITY 2 Interpret Behaviors

1 Misunderstandings happen when we don't understand why people from different cultures act the way they do. Look at the student behaviors in the chart. List possible reasons why the person is behaving that way. The first item is completed as an example.

Student Behavior	Possible Reasons
1. doesn't look at other people when speaking	-it is rude in the student's culture -student lacks confidence -student is dishonest -student dislikes person she is speaking to
2. constantly apologizes	
3. shrugs shoulders when asked questions	
4. always sits away from everyone else	
5. usually sits way in the back of the classroom	
6. says "yes" to everything	
7. gives opinions without being asked	
8. never gives opinions, even when asked	
9. asks lots of questions	
10. acts embarrassed when called on by the teacher	
11. does not participate in class discussions	

2 Work in small groups. Share the reasons you listed for each behavior in the chart. Then discuss these questions:

a. Were you surprised by your classmates' reasons for a behavior? Why?

b. If there were differences in the reasons you and your classmates listed, were they caused by differences in culture or by something else?

III. Presentation Preview

When people travel to another country to sightsee, study, or live, they need to learn many new customs and behaviors. Your project is to give a two- to three-minute speech about a situation in which you or someone you know experienced a culture conflict.

ACTIVITY 1 **Listen to a Model Presentation**

Listen to a model speech about Taj's culture conflict.

MODEL SPEECH: Making Tea

INTRODUCTION

I'm holding a tea bag. I'm sure most of you have seen one of these before. They are very popular in the United States. Using a tea bag is a good way to make tea. You are probably thinking, "Why is Taj showing us a tea bag? How can a tea bag cause a culture conflict?"

Statement of Culture Conflict

Well, a tea bag caused me to experience a culture conflict that was very embarrassing.

BODY

I will now *get to the point*. The first school I went to in the United States was the University of Florida. My new American friend, Susan, invited me to have lunch with her and her friends in the school cafeteria.

* *Tell the most important information*

I ordered a cup of tea from the woman serving the food. In India, I never used a tea bag. My mother always made fresh tea using tea leaves. I tore open the tea bag and put the tea leaves into my cup of hot water.

Susan looked at me and said, "Oh no! Taj, don't drink that!" I was afraid to say anything because I didn't want *to put my foot in my mouth*. Susan got me another cup of hot water and a new tea bag. She showed me how to dip the tea bag in the water. Then I told Susan I liked my tea sweet, so she gave me a paper packet of sugar. Before Susan could stop me, I put the packet of sugar in the hot water like this.

* *Say something embarrassing*

Her friends started to laugh. Susan told me not to drink the tea, but I didn't understand why. Susan explained that first, I should tear open the sugar packet, second, put the sugar into the tea, and third, throw away the paper. I thought she was trying to *pull the wool over my eyes*. Then she *pulled some strings* and got me another cup of hot water and tea bag for free.

* *Trick me*
* *Used her influence*

I was confused. It didn't make sense to me. I was supposed to dip the tea bag into my cup without tearing it open, but I was supposed to tear open the sugar packet before putting the sugar in my tea?

CONCLUSION

At the time I was upset. I felt silly because the other people at the table were laughing. Now I understand how funny it looked to them. I know that if any of you ever come to visit me in India, you, too, will experience a culture conflict. I will try not to laugh at you!

Thank you for listening and allowing me to share my very frustrating culture conflict with you.

1 Listen to Taj's Culture Conflict speech again. Then answer the questions about the speech.

1. What did Taj say he was holding?

   _____

2. What was the name of the first school Taj attended in the United States?

   _____

3. Where did Susan invite Taj to have lunch?

   _____

4. What did Taj order to drink?

   _____

5. What did Taj do with the tea bag?

   _____

6. What did Susan say when she saw what Taj did with the tea bag?

   _____

7. Why was Taj afraid to speak?

   _____

8. What did Susan show Taj how to do?

   _____

9. What did Taj do with the packet of sugar?

   _____

10. What did Susan explain to Taj about using sugar packets?

    First, _____

    Second, _____

    Third, _____

ACTIVITY 3 Model Speech Discussion

Discuss these questions in small groups.

1. Was Taj's culture conflict a good speech topic? Why or why not?
2. Was his attention getter effective? Why or why not?
3. What was his culture conflict?
4. What details did he use in the body of his speech to explain his conflict?
5. Was his use of speech aids effective? Why?
6. How did Taj conclude his speech?

IV. Pronunciation Practice: [u] and [ʊ]

A common error is to confuse the vowel sounds [u] (as in *suit*) and [ʊ] (as in *soot.*) If you confuse these sounds, *pool* sounds like *pull* and *full* sounds like *fool!*

The sound [u] is long and stressed. When you pronounce [u], push out your lips as if you were going to whistle or kiss someone. The sound [ʊ] is short and relaxed. Your lips barely move.

ACTIVITY 1 Contrast Words with [u] and [ʊ]

Listen and repeat the following word pairs. Be sure to push your lips into a "kiss" when you pronounce long [u]. Relax your lips when you say short [ʊ].

[u]	[ʊ]
1. pool	pull
2. fool	full
3. suit	soot
4. Luke	look
5. stewed	stood

> **PRONUNCIATION TIPS**
>
> The letter *u* followed by *sh* is usually pronounced [ʊ].
>
> Examples: bush, push, cushion
>
> The letters *oo* followed by *d* or *k* are usually pronounced [ʊ].
>
> Examples: good, wood, book, cooking

ACTIVITY 2 Practice Sentences

Listen and repeat the following sentences aloud. Be sure to pronounce the [u] and [ʊ] words carefully.

    [ʊ]   [u]
1. Pull him from the pool.

          [ʊ] [ʊ]   [u]
2. Take a good look at Luke.

          [ʊ]   [u] [u] [u]
3. He has soot on his new blue suit.

            [ʊ]   [u]
4. The horse should be shoed.

            [ʊ]   [u] [ʊ] [ʊ]   [u]
5. The table is full of beautiful-looking food.

ACTIVITY 3   Identify Words with [u] and [ʊ]

🎧 **1** Listen again to Taj's Model Speech on page 89. Circle eleven words pronounced with [u] and underline twelve words pronounced with [ʊ]. Write the words in the chart. The first word appears as an example.

Words with [u]	Words with [ʊ]
you	

2 Take turns pronouncing the lists of words with a partner.

ACTIVITY 4   Practice the Model Speech

With a partner, take turns reading the Model Speech on page 89 aloud. Pay attention to your pronunciation of [u] and [ʊ]. (Remember, push out your lips as you say [u]. Your lips should hardly move as you pronounce [ʊ].)

V.   Playing with Sayings: Sayings with [u] and [ʊ]

ACTIVITY 1   Learn the Meanings

A Read the following sayings. Place a checkmark (✓) next to those you heard in the Model Speech.

_____ 1. **Too good to be true:** probably not real because it's too perfect
The man said I could earn a thousand dollars a week without working. That sounds *too good to be true.*

_____ 2. **Pull the wool over one's eyes:** to trick or fool someone
My teacher didn't believe my excuse. I couldn't *pull the wool over her eyes.*

_____ 3. **Put one's foot in one's mouth:** to say something silly or embarrassing
Think before you speak so you don't *put your foot in your mouth.*

_____ 4. **Get to the point:** to tell the most important information quickly
I am in a hurry so please *get to the point.*

_____ 5. **Pull some strings:** to use influence to get what you need
My friend *pulled some strings* and got me a job in his office.

B Circle the [u] sounds in the sayings in Activity 1. Underline the [ʊ] sounds. Pronounce each word out loud several times.

C Match the idioms with their meanings.

_____ 1. get to the point   a. to say something foolish

_____ 2. pull some strings   b. to use influence

_____ 3. pull the wool over one's eyes   c. to trick someone

_____ 4. too good to be true   d. to get to the important topic

_____ 5. put one's foot in one's mouth   e. too wonderful to be real

ACTIVITY 2   **Use the Sayings**

A Fill in the blanks with the correct saying.

1. **Friend:** I need two tickets to the movies on Tuesday. Can you get me a discount?

   You: Sure. I know the owner of the movie theatre. I will _____

   and get you the tickets.

2. **Friend:** I told my parents I was going out to buy a book but I'm really going to a party.

   You: Come on, your parents are too smart to believe that. It's not so easy to

   _____.

3. **Friend:** My cousin promised to give me a new car and buy my gas for a year.

   You: That's great, but it sounds _____.

4. **Friend:** So how do you like my idea?

   You: You haven't told me your idea yet. You need to _____.

5. **Friend:** Sometimes, I say things without thinking about them first.

   You: I know. You need to learn how to think before you speak. You don't want to

   _____.

B Practice reading the short dialogues in pairs. Pay attention to the pronunciation of [u] and [ʊ].

C Work with a partner. Write your own two-line dialogues. Use a different saying in each one. Then work with another pair of students. Take turns reading your dialogues aloud.

VI. Presentation Project: A Culture Conflict

Your project is to prepare and present a speech about a culture conflict that you or someone you know has experienced.

STEP 1 | Choose a Topic

Choose a custom related to one of the following situations, the situations in Activity 1: Describe Customs on page 86, or another situation you have experienced.

speaking a new language	clothing styles
eating customs	rules about personal space
using local telephones	giving or receiving a gift
using banking machines	giving compliments
waiting in a line	using public transportation

A Read the instructions for organizing your speech.

Introduction
1. Include an attention-getting opener.
2. State your culture conflict.

Body
Provide details about your conflict.
1. What happened?
2. Where were you? What were you doing?
3. When did it happen?
4. Why were you there? Who was with you?
5. How did you and other people react?
6. Did anyone try to help you? How?
7. How did the situation end?

Conclusion
1. Make a final statement(s) your audience will remember.
2. Thank your audience for listening to you.

B Fill in the Speech Preparation Worksheet on page 95. You may change some questions or add your own.

C Read the Useful Language expressions you can use to begin the body of your speech. Place a checkmark (✓) next to the expressions you like best.

USEFUL LANGUAGE: BEGINNING THE BODY OF THE SPEECH

_____ Let me tell you what happened. I was . . .

_____ I will now describe how _____ caused my culture conflict.

_____ I'm sure you're wondering what happened. I will now *get to the point!*

Speech Preparation Worksheet: A Culture Conflict

_____

INTRODUCTION

_____

Attention-Getter

_____

Statement of Culture Conflict

BODY

1. What happened?	
2. Where were you? What were you doing?	
3. When did it happen?	
4. Why were you there? Who was with you?	
5. How did you react to what happened?	
6. How did the people around you react?	
7. Did anyone try to help you? Who? How?	
8. How did the situation end?	
9.	
10.	

CONCLUSION

_____

Final Statement(s)

_____

Thank the audience

_____

D Select a saying from page 92 to include in your speech. Write it here: _____

E Include at least one speech aid.

STEP 3 | Prepare Note Cards

A Use the guidelines in step 2A, page 94, to prepare note cards for your speech. Label the cards Introduction, Body, and Conclusion.

B Fill in details from your Speech Preparation Worksheet. Use as many cards as you need.

C Add Useful Language expressions from page 94 and a saying from page 92 to your notes.

D Note where you will present your speech aids.

E Number your cards.

STEP 4 | Practice Your Speech

A Practice your speech in front of a mirror using your note cards and speech aids. Record the speech and listen to it at least once. Make sure it is two to three minutes long.

B Complete the Speech Checklist. Is there anything you want to change or improve before you present it in class?

Speech Checklist	YES	NO
1. In my introduction I included an attention-getting opener and stated my culture conflict.	☐	☐
2. I included details about my culture conflict.	☐	☐
3. I prepared a conclusion and thanked the audience for listening.	☐	☐
4. I included a speech aid.	☐	☐
5. I included a saying from the chapter.	☐	☐
6. I included a Useful Language expression.	☐	☐
7. My pronunciation of [u] and [ʊ] is correct.	☐	☐
8. My speech is two to three minutes long.	☐	☐

C Practice again with your note cards and speech aids.

D Your teacher and/or your classmates may evaluate your speech. Study the form on page 146 so you know how you will be evaluated. You may use the items on the form to make final changes to your speech.

STEP 5 | Present Your Speech

A Relax, take a deep breath, and present your speech.

B Listen to your audience's applause.

CHAPTER 8

CONVINCE ME!

Have you ever tried to convince someone to do something he or she didn't want to do? Have you ever tried to convince your family members to believe something they didn't think was true? Has anyone ever tried to change your mind about something? Well, this is what persuasion is all about—convincing others to change their opinion to agree with yours or to do what you want them to do.

CHAPTER CHALLENGE Your challenge in this chapter is to convince listeners to change a belief or behavior. By the time you complete this chapter, you will be able to:

- identify persuasive situations
- decide whether your purpose is to change someone's belief or behavior
- plan, prepare, and present a persuasive speech using Monroe's Motivated Sequence

I. Decide Your Purpose

Before you can attempt to change someone's mind or persuade a person to do something, you need to decide exactly what you want him or her to believe or do. There are two general purposes of speaking to persuade:

- to convince people to agree with you about something
- to convince people to take action or change a behavior (either begin a new behavior or stop an old one)

The activities in this section will help you decide the purpose of your speech.

ACTIVITY 1 Identify the Purpose

1 Read the following statements. Is their purpose (a) to change a belief or (b) to persuade people to change their behavior or take an action? Check the correct box.

Statements	Change Belief	Take Action/ Change Behavior
1. The U.S. is the best place to study English.		
2. Buy a smoke detector for every room in your house.		
3. Children should be allowed to watch any TV show they want.		
4. Don't talk on a cell phone when you drive.		
5. People should not get married before age 25.		
6. All college students should perform community service.		
7. Don't use any product tested on animals.		
8. Always wear a helmet when riding a bicycle.		
9. Use public transportation instead of driving to school.		
10. Eat fish instead of meat.		

2 Compare your answers in small groups. Then discuss these questions.

1. Which statements do you agree with? Give reasons.
2. Which statements do you disagree with? Give reasons.

1 List situations when you tried to convince someone (or someone tried to convince you) to change a belief or take some action. Write them in the chart.

Change a Belief	Take an Action/Change a Behavior
EXAMPLE: I tried to convince my brother that English is not a difficult language.	**EXAMPLE:** I tried to convince my parents to buy me a motorcycle.

2 Share your situations in small groups. Discuss these questions.

a. What was the situation?

b. What arguments did you use to try to convince your listeners?

c. Did the other person disagree with these arguments? How?

d. Did you succeed in changing your listener's opinion or behavior? Explain.

EXAMPLE:

I tried to convince my parents to buy me a motorcycle. My arguments were:

- They wouldn't have to drive me to school anymore.
- It would save a lot of money on gas.

My parents argued:

- Motorcycles aren't safe.
- They couldn't afford the necessary insurance.

In the end, they did not buy me a motorcycle, so I did not convince them to take an action.

II. The Motivated Sequence

Professor Alan H. Monroe developed this very popular method to convince others to change their opinions or behaviors. Speakers have used this method of persuasion for over eighty years!

STEP 1 | Attention Step

You need to get your listeners' attention right away. There are several ways to do this:

1. Begin with an unexpected visual aid.
   EXAMPLE:
   Hold up a vial of blood.

2. Tell some startling statistics.
   EXAMPLE:
   "1,000 people die every hour because…"

3. Tell a unique story.

EXAMPLE:

"My sister almost died last week. She was saved by…"

4. Begin with a question, or present a powerful quotation.

EXAMPLE:

Would you like to save someone's life today?

STEP 2 | Need Step

Show the listeners there is a serious problem and something must be done about it.

1. Present proof there is a need.

EXAMPLE:

According to the American Red Cross, there is a severe shortage of blood.

2. Give statistics that prove there is a need.

EXAMPLE:

Due to the blood shortage, 8.5 million people die every year.

STEP 3 | Satisfaction Step

Tell your audience how to meet the need or solve the problem.

1. Give your solution to the problem.

EXAMPLE:

You can help solve the blood shortage problem by donating blood today after class at the blood mobile parked outside.

2. Explain how your solution will solve the problem.

EXAMPLE:

Your donation will help reduce the blood shortage and save lives.

STEP 4 | Visualization Step

Get your audience to visualize—to "see"—the benefits of your solution.

1. Help them imagine all the wonderful things that will happen if they do what you want.

EXAMPLE:

Show photos of children who will live if they receive blood.

2. Convince them that bad things will happen if they don't follow your advice.

EXAMPLE:

Show pictures of people who will die without blood.

STEP 5 | Action Step

Encourage your audience to take a specific action or actions. (Note: Speakers often use imperative verbs in this part of their presentation.)

1. Be brief and specific.

EXAMPLES:

Donate blood, email your senators, vote for the candidate, sign the petition

2. End strong:

EXAMPLE:

Don't wait! Hurry to the blood mobile parked outside.

ACTIVITY Analyze the Information

1 **Work with a partner. Analyze the following statements from a persuasive speech about organ donation. Label each statement (Attention, Need, Satisfaction, Visualization, Action) according to its place in Monroe's Motivated Sequence.**

EXAMPLE:

I'm passing around organ donor cards. Please fill one out and put it in your wallet right now!
Action

a. *"Give my sight to the man who has never seen a sunrise. Give my heart to a person whose heart has caused nothing but endless days of pain."* (From a poem by Robert Test)

   _____

b. A seventeen-year-old in Wisconsin died in a car accident. His mom donated his organs. His heart went to a priest; his kidneys went to a mother of five children and another seventeen-year-old boy. Now imagine how YOUR organs could benefit so many deserving people. Think of the comfort your family would have knowing that you live on in others. _____

c. Over 100,000 people are waiting for an organ in the United States. Eighteen people die each day because they haven't received a needed organ. _____

d. You can help solve the organ shortage by donating your organs when you die. Organ donation benefits both the donor's family and the recipients. _____

e. Tonight when you go home, tell your family that you want to be an organ donor after you die. _____

2 **Compare your answers in small groups.**

III. Presentation Preview

Your goal is to choose a topic you feel strongly about and to plan and prepare a speech to convince your listeners to agree with you, take action, or make a change.

ACTIVITY 1 Listen to the Model Speech

Listen to Krista's model speech. Pay attention to each step of the Motivated Sequence.

MODEL SPEECH: Give the Gift of Life

[Attention Step]

[The speaker, Krista, holds up a vial of a liquid that looks like blood.]

- Without this, someone dies every 3¾ seconds.
- Without this, sixteen people die every minute.
- Without this, 1,000 people die every hour.
- Without this, 8.5 million people die every year.

Out of the blue, without warning, you or a loved one could be among them!

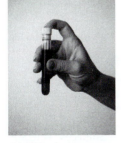

vial of blood

* *suddenly*

What is this? This is blood.

Now that I have your attention, I want you to listen carefully while I tell you about a big problem in the United States.

(continued)

(Continued)

[Need Step]

According to the American Red Cross, there is a shortage of blood. In other words, blood centers don't have enough blood to meet the needs of patients in hospitals and clinics. That's because less than 5 percent of people who are healthy enough to give blood actually donate blood to blood banks.

Unless more people become blood donors, the supply of blood will NOT be enough to help everyone who needs it. That could include you!

[Satisfaction Step]

Today you have a golden opportunity to help save lives. By donating blood at the blood mobile parked outside this building, you can help reduce the serious blood shortage!

[Visualization Step]

Think of the lives you could save:

- Your donation of only ONE pint can save up to four lives.

- You could save the lives of a child's grandmother and grandfather.

- You could save the lives of a brother and a sister.

- You could save the life of a baby.

Someday, YOUR life might depend on being able to receive blood. I'll say this *in black and white*: Make sure that blood will be there if and when YOU need it!

* very clearly

[Action Step]

Don't wait. Hurry to the bloodmobile parked outside. Give blood now and invite a friend to donate blood with you. Remember, the life you save may be your own!

🎧 **1** **Listen to Krista's speech again and complete the outline.**

Attention Step

I. Without blood many people die.

    A. Someone dies every 3¾ seconds.

    B. _____

    C. 1,000 people die every _____

    D. _____ year

II. Now that I have your attention, I want you to listen carefully while I tell you about _____.

Need Step

I. _____

    A. Blood centers don't have enough blood to meet patients' needs in:

       1. hospitals

       2. _____

    B. _____

    C. The _____ is not enough to help everyone who needs it.

II. That could include you!

Satisfaction Step

I. Today, you have a _____to help save lives.

II. By donating blood, _____

Visualization Step

I. Think of the lives you could save.

    A. One pint can save up to four lives.

    B. _____

    C. You could save a brother and sister.

    D. _____

II. Someday, your life might depend on being able to receive blood.

Action Step

I. _____

    A. Give blood now_____

    B. _____

II. Remember, the life you save _____!

2 **Work with a partner and compare your completed outlines.**

ACTIVITY 3 **Model Presentation Discussion**

Discuss these questions in small groups.

1. What was the topic of Krista's speech?
2. Was her purpose to get you to change an opinion or take an action?
3. Was her speech well-researched? How do you know?
4. What was the most persuasive part of Krista's speech?
5. Was Krista's Attention Step effective? Why or why not?
6. What information does Krista give in the Need step of her speech?
7. How does Krista's solution help solve the problem?
8. How did Krista use visualization to convince you to donate blood?
9. How does Krista conclude her speech? Do you think this a strong ending? Why or why not?

IV. Pronunciation Practice: [b], [v], and [w]

A common error is to pronounce the sound [b] or [w] like [v], or to pronounce [v] like [b] or [w]. If you confuse [b] and [v], *vote* sounds like *boat* and *best* sounds like *vest*. If you confuse [w] and [v], *wine* sounds like *vine* and *vet* sounds like *wet*.

To pronounce [b], press your lips together firmly. To pronounce [v], place your top teeth over your bottom lip. To pronounce [w], round your lips as if you were going to whistle. Don't let your lower lip touch your upper teeth!

ACTIVITY 1 **Word Practice**

 Listen and repeat the following sets of words.

[b]	[v]	[w]
1. be	V	we
2. bet	vet	wet
3. bow	vow	wow
4. best	vest	west
5. bent	vent	went

ACTIVITY 2 **Sentence Practice**

 Listen and repeat the following sentences.

1. The **berry** tastes **very** sweet.
2. **Walt** lost his key to the **vault**.
3. **Of** course, a **whale would** look silly **wearing** a **veil**.
4. **Victor bought one bun** at the **bakery**.
5. The **waiter bent** the metal **vent**.

> **PRONUNCIATION TIPS**
>
> • The "f" in the word "o_f_" is pronounced [v].
> • The "o" in the word "_o_ne" is pronounced [w].

1 Listen again to Krista's model speech on pages 101 and 102. Circle all the words pronounced with [b], [v], and [w]. Write the words in the chart.

Words with [b] (18)		Words with [v] (10)		Words with [w] (14)	

2 Take turns pronouncing the lists of words with a partner.

ACTIVITY 4 Practice the Model Speech

Now take turns reading the Model Speech on pages 101–102 aloud with your partner. Be sure to pronounce the words with [b], [v], and [w] correctly.

V. Playing with Sayings: Sayings with [b], [v], and [w]

ACTIVITY 1 Learn the Meanings

1 Read the following sayings and their meanings. Check (✓) the ones you heard in Krista's Model Speech.

_____   a. **With bells on:** to do something with great joy or enthusiasm
I will attend my best friend's party *with bells on!*

_____   b. **Wear out one's welcome:** to stay too long
He *wore out his welcome* by staying a week instead of a few days.

_____   c. **White lie:** a lie that is not serious
The woman told a *white lie.* She said she was twenty-one years old instead of twenty-five!

_____   d. **Out of the blue:** unexpectedly, without warning
After fifteen years of no communication, my uncle called me *out of the blue.*

_____   e. **In black and white:** very clearly, in a way that's very easy way to understand
The teacher explained the rules in *black and white.*

2 Match the idioms with their synonyms. Then compare your answers with a partner's.

_____ 1. with bells on   a. become annoying

_____ 2. wear out one's welcome   b. suddenly

_____ 3. white lie   c. clearly

_____ 4. out of the blue   d. a minor untruth

_____ 5. in black and white   e. happily

ACTIVITY 2   **Use the Sayings**

1 Complete the following sentences with your own ideas.

a. I will go to _____with bells on.

b. He _wore out his welcome_ because _____.

c. Silvi told a _white lie_ when she said _____.

d. (Describe an event that happened)_____ _out of the blue._

e. I hope you can _____in black and white.

2 Practice reading your sentences in small groups. Pay attention to the pronunciation of [b], [v], and [w].

VI. Presentation Project: Convince Me!

Think of an issue that you have a strong opinion about. Decide whether you want to:

- change your classmates' beliefs about the issue
- persuade them to take action
- persuade them to change a behavior or habit

Your project is to prepare and present a three- to four-minute speech about the issue. Your goal is to convince as many people as possible to agree with your opinion or to do what you want them to do.

STEP 1 | Choose a Topic

Choose one of the following topics, a topic from Activity 1: Identify the Purpose on page 98, or another topic.

Parrots make wonderful pets.	Floss your teeth daily.
Every child should have a pet.	Sign an organ donor card today.
Enroll in a photography class.	Use sun block when you go to the beach.
Marijuana should be legalized.	Always use seatbelts in a car.
Buy a hybrid car.	Donate to your favorite charity.
Stop eating red meat.	The legal drinking age should be 18.
Drunk drivers should lose their licenses.	High school students should be required to wear uniforms.
Eat sweet potatoes instead of white potatoes.	

A Review the five steps for organizing your speech.

Attention Step
- Begin with an unexpected visual aid.
- Tell some startling facts or statistics.
- Tell a unique story.
- Begin with a question or present a famous quotation.

Need Step
- Present facts showing there is a need.
- Give statistics that prove there is a need.

Satisfaction Step
- Give your solution to the problem.
- Explain how your solution will solve the problem.

Visualization Step
- Convince your audience to see the benefits of your plan.
- Convince your audience that bad things will happen if they don't agree with you.

Action Step (Tell your audience to do something specific)
- Use imperative verbs.
- Include a strong final sentence.

B Read the Useful Language expressions you can use to get your listeners' attention. Place a checkmark (✓) next to the ones you like best.

> **USEFUL LANGUAGE: ATTENTION GETTERS**
>
> _____ You might be shocked to learn…[surprising fact].
>
> _____ Did you know that…[surprising fact]?
>
> _____ Raise your hands if you've ever…[done something related to the speech].
>
> _____ [A famous person] once said…"[quote]."
>
> _____ Imagine this: [Imaginary situation.]

C Complete the following outline for your speech.

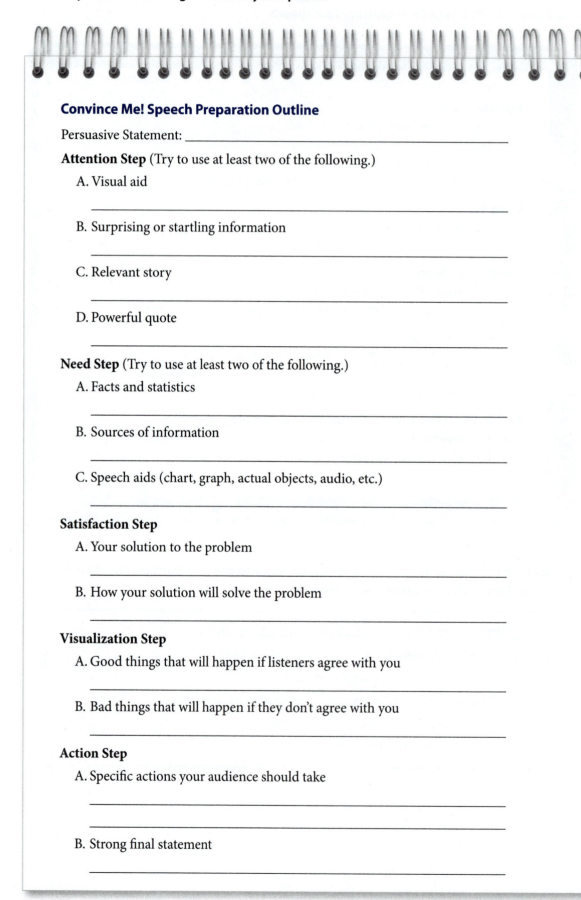

Convince Me! Speech Preparation Outline

Persuasive Statement: _____

Attention Step (Try to use at least two of the following.)

   A. Visual aid

   _____

   B. Surprising or startling information

   _____

   C. Relevant story

   _____

   D. Powerful quote

   _____

Need Step (Try to use at least two of the following.)

   A. Facts and statistics

   _____

   B. Sources of information

   _____

   C. Speech aids (chart, graph, actual objects, audio, etc.)

   _____

Satisfaction Step

   A. Your solution to the problem

   _____

   B. How your solution will solve the problem

   _____

Visualization Step

   A. Good things that will happen if listeners agree with you

   _____

   B. Bad things that will happen if they don't agree with you

   _____

Action Step

   A. Specific actions your audience should take

   _____

   _____

   B. Strong final statement

   _____

D Prepare at least one speech aid.

E Select a saying from page 105 to include in your speech. Write it here: _____.

STEP 3 | Prepare Note Cards

A Review the five steps on page 105 and prepare note cards for your speech. Label the cards:

- Attention
- Need
- Satisfaction
- Visualization
- Action

B Fill in details from your Speech Preparation Outline. Use as many cards as you need.

C Add Useful Language from page 107 and a saying from page 105 to your notes.

D Number your cards.

STEP 4 | Practice Your Speech

A Practice your speech with your note cards and speech aid. Record it and listen to it at least once. Be sure it is three to four minutes long.

B Complete the Speech Checklist. Is there anything you want to change or improve before you present it in class?

Speech Checklist	YES	NO
1. I included the Attention step.	☐	☐
2. I included the Need step.	☐	☐
3. I included the Satisfaction step.	☐	☐
4. I included the Visualization step.	☐	☐
5. I included the Action step.	☐	☐
6. I included a saying from the chapter.	☐	☐
7. I included a speech aid.	☐	☐
8. I included a Useful Language expression.	☐	☐
9. My pronunciation of words with [b], [v], and [w] is clear.	☐	☐
10. My speech is 3 to 4 minutes long.	☐	☐

C Practice one or two more times with your note cards and speech aid(s).

D Your teacher and/or your classmates may evaluate your speech. Study the form on page 147 so you know how you will be evaluated. You may use the items on the form to make final changes to your speech.

STEP 5 | Present Your Speech

A Relax, take a deep breath, and present your speech.

B Listen to your audience's applause.

CHAPTER 9

LET'S DISCUSS IT!

We can't have a discussion by ourselves! In order to discuss a topic, two or more people must participate. We participate in discussions all the time: at home with our families, in class with our classmates, at work with co-workers or bosses, or at parties with friends. Learning how to contribute to a discussion is an important communication skill.

CHAPTER CHALLENGE Your challenge in this chapter is to plan and prepare for a discussion about a topic that interests all the members of a small group. By the time you complete this chapter, you will be able to:

- brainstorm ideas and select the best ones
- lead a group discussion
- research a topic and contribute to a discussion about it

I. Brainstorming

Brainstorming means listing as many ideas as you can think of about a topic and then selecting the best ones. Brainstorming in a group encourages participation, helps group members develop new ways of looking at an issue, and reminds people that others have interesting and creative ideas also.

A. Brainstorming Ideas

Read the following suggestions for brainstorming in groups.

- Write your topic on a piece of paper.
- Say anything about the topic that you think of, even if it seems very silly.
- Listen to the other group members and list all the ideas that they contribute. Write quickly; grammar is not important at this time!
- Don't talk about the ideas; just write them down without discussing them.

ACTIVITY 1 **Practice Brainstorming**

1 Work with four or five classmates. Read the following situation.

Dakar is always asking his friend Rudy to loan him money. He usually "forgets" to pay Rudy back. Rudy needs excuses why he can't loan Dakar any more money.

2 Brainstorm excuses that Rudy can give Dakar for not loaning him money. (Use your imagination; it's OK to be silly!) Try to think of at least ten ideas. Be sure that everyone in the group contributes.

EXAMPLES:

A pickpocket stole my wallet this morning in the parking lot.

I gave all my money to a homeless man today.

a. _____

b. _____

c. _____

d. _____

e. _____

f. _____

g. _____

h. _____

i. _____

j. _____

3 Discuss the advantages and disadvantages of each excuse.

4 Choose the three best excuses. Write them here:

a. _____

b. _____

c. _____

Choose the Best Ideas

1 Each group will share its three best excuses from Activity 1 with the class. One student from each group should write the group's ideas on the board.

2 One student will lead a class discussion about the advantages and disadvantages of all the excuses listed on the board.

3 The student will ask the class to vote for its three favorite ideas.

II. Responsibilities of Group Members

When working together, members of a group have responsibilities toward one another. In order for a group discussion to be a success, group members need to practice certain behaviors during the discussion.

ACTIVITY 1 **Identify Responsibilities of Group Members**

Work in small groups. Read the following list of behaviors. Check seven behaviors that you should follow when participating in a discussion.

_____ 1. Interrupt another group member if you have something important to say

_____ 2. Listen carefully to what the other group members say

_____ 3. Say anything that pops into your head at any point in the discussion

_____ 4. Look up words in a dictionary while a group member is speaking

_____ 5. Ask follow-up questions if you would like more information

_____ 6. Refer to all group members by name

_____ 7. Ignore your group members when they are speaking

_____ 8. Make comments about what another group member said

_____ 9. Be prepared with information about the discussion topic

_____ 10. Contribute many times during the discussion

ACTIVITY 2 **Identify Group Leader Responsibilities**

Work with a different small group of classmates. Read the list of responsibilities. Check six responsibilities of the leader during a group discussion.

_____ 1. Introduce the topic and participants

_____ 2. Control and dominate the conversation

_____ 3. Get the discussion started

_____ 4. Encourage all group members to participate

_____ 5. Criticize group members who are not prepared

_____ 6. Provide transitions between each part of the discussion

_____ 7. End the discussion when the time is up

_____ 8. Thank the participants for their hard work

ACTIVITY 3 **Discuss Group Members' and Leaders' Responsibilities**

Discuss the following questions as a class.

1. Who has been in a group discussion? What was the situation? What was the topic of the discussion?

2. Was the discussion well organized? Why or why not?

3. Which of the seven behaviors you checked in Activity 1 did group members demonstrate?

4. Which of the six guidelines you checked in Activity 2 did the group leader follow?

5. Which behaviors do you agree/disagree with? Why?

6. Can you think of any other behaviors group members or leaders should demonstrate? What are they?

III. Presentation Preview

Your goal with your classmates is to choose a law, government regulation, or rule that exists anywhere in the world and participate in a discussion about it.

ACTIVITY 1 **Listen to the Model Discussion**

Listen to the Model Discussion called "Gum Chewing in Singapore." Pay attention to each step of the discussion.

MODEL DISCUSSION: Gum Chewing in Singapore

INTRODUCTION BY GROUP LEADER	**Karina:**	Good morning, everyone. As you all know, today our group is going to discuss the law that bans chewing gum in Singapore. We'll describe the law and talk about why it was passed. Then we'll discuss the penalties for breaking the law. Finally, we'll all share our personal opinions about it. Is everyone ready?
	Jorge, Karim, Keiko: }	Yes
Group Leader Transition	**Karina:**	All right. Let's begin by describing the law. Who wants to start? [Jorge raises his hand.] OK. Great, Jorge.
DETAILS ABOUT THE LAW	**Jorge:**	I first read about this law in the *Miami Herald*. I was really surprised to read that it's illegal to chew gum in Singapore. I couldn't believe it.
	Keiko:	I couldn't believe it either. However, I read that nicotine gum is legal.
	Karim:	Nicotine gum? What's that?
	Jorge:	It's a special kind of gum to help people stop smoking. As Keiko said, nicotine gum is legal.
	Karina:	Oh, that's interesting, Jorge. I didn't read about that. I'd like to add that it's also against the law to bring gum into Singapore or sell it there.
	Karim:	That's true. I read in the *Sunday Times Online* that travelers aren't allowed to bring even small amounts of gum into the country.
	Karina:	Can anyone add to what Karim said?
	Keiko:	I can. I read a similar story in the *Sydney Morning Herald* online. It said that adults and kids going to Singapore should be sure not to have chewing gum in their pockets, briefcases, or handbags.
	Karina:	Does anyone know how long this law has been *on the books*?
	Jorge:	I do. Since 1992!
	Karina:	Wow! That's really interesting. Good work finding that!
Group Leader Transition	**Karina:**	OK, now that we know the details of the law, let's talk about the reasons why the government passed it.
REASONS FOR THE LAW	**Karina:**	Who has information about why this law was passed?
	Karim:	There's a really bad punishment for breaking the law.
	Karina:	Wait a moment, Karim, we'll talk about penalties for breaking the law later. Right now, we need to stay on topic. We're talking about the reasons for the law.
	Karim:	Oh, sorry! It was to keep the city clean.
	Karina:	Could you be a little more specific?
	Karim:	Sure. The government didn't want people to stick their gum on chairs and under tables in public places.

* Part of the law

	Keiko:	That's true. They also didn't like having chewing gum all over the floors of the buses.
	Jorge:	I learned about another reason. It seems that gum caused delays on Singapore's subway trains.
	Karim:	I don't understand. How could gum cause delays?
	Jorge:	Well, people stuck gum on the doors and then they couldn't close. And it cost a lot of money to fix the doors.
	Karina:	That's a good point, Jorge. I read that it was costing the government hundreds of thousands of dollars a year to remove the gum from public areas.
	Keiko:	Wow. That's a lot of money.
Group Leader Transition	**Karina:**	All right, everyone has made some good points about why this law was created. Now we need to *make tracks* so we don't run out of time. Let's talk about what happens to people who break the law. Who has information about that?
PENALTIES FOR BREAKING THE LAW	**Keiko:**	I do. A person can receive a fine of $500 to $1000 if it's their first time.
	Karina:	That's really expensive. I saw a CNBC video on YouTube about another penalty. A gum chewer can also get something called a "CWO."
	Karim:	What's a CWO ?
	Karina:	A Corrective Work Order. It means a judge forces the person to wear a brightly colored jacket and clean public places.
	Keiko:	That's true, Karina. But that's not all. I also learned that if you're caught chewing gum, the TV and newspapers are invited to report on it. They might put a picture of you on the evening news!
	Jorge:	That's awful. It would be so embarrassing. If that happened to me, I would try to *pull some strings* to get out of it.
	Karina:	I would too, Jorge! Unfortunately, I don't think it would do much good. Singapore is very strict. If you break their laws, you get punished for sure.
Group Leader Transition	**Karina:**	OK. Let's summarize. So far we've discussed the law, the reasons for it, and the penalties for breaking it. Now let's take turns giving our opinions.
OPINIONS	**Karina:**	Keiko, let's start with you. What's your opinion?
	Keiko:	I like the law. It helps to reduce the amount of trash. I've been to Singapore, and I can tell you it's one of the cleanest cities in the world.
	Karina:	Do you all agree with Keiko?
	Jorge:	I agree because I don't like stepping in gum and getting it all over my shoes.
	Karim:	Would you like to know what I think?
	Karina:	Of course, Karim. We're *all ears*!
	Karim:	I disagree with Keiko and Jorge. I think the law is way too strict. If I got arrested, I'm sure I would *go to pieces*.
	Karina:	I disagree with the law too. Chewing gum shouldn't be forbidden completely. People who don't throw their gum in the garbage should pay a fine. But they shouldn't get fined just for chewing it.
	Jorge:	That's a good point, Karina. I agree with you. Singapore doesn't ban cigarettes, and they make the streets dirty, too. If they ban gum, they should ban cigarettes, fast food wrappers, and anything else that people could throw on the ground.
	Keiko:	Jorge, that's so true. I never thought of that!
CONCLUSION BY GROUP LEADER	**Karina:**	Well everyone, our time is up. We've heard a lot of interesting facts and ideas this morning. Thank you all for participating.

* Hurry

* Use one's connection to important people

Keiko showed this photo.

* Listening carefully

* Become terribly upset and unable to function

1 Listen to the discussion again and write the answers to the questions.

Details about the Law

a. What law did the group discuss?

_____

b. What type of gum is legal in Singapore?

_____

c. What did Karim read in the *Sunday Times Online*?

_____

d. How long has Singapore had this law?

_____

Reasons for the Law

e. What was the main purpose of the law?

_____

f. Where did people keep sticking their gum?

_____

g. How did chewing gum cause delays on Singapore's trains?

_____

h. How much did it cost the government to clean up the gum from public places?

_____

Penalties for Breaking the Law

i. What is the fine for a first-time offender?

_____

j. What does "CWO" stand for?

_____

k. What would Jorge do if he received a CWO?

_____

Opinions

l. Why does Keiko like the law?

_____

m. What does Karim think about the law?

_____

n. How does Karina feel about the law?

_____

2 Work with a partner and compare answers.

ACTIVITY 3 Analyze the Model Discussion

Discuss these questions in small groups.

1. Was this discussion well organized? Why or why not?
2. Did all group members participate actively?
3. Did all group members research the topic? How do you know?
4. Did group members listen carefully to each other? How do you know?
5. Did the group leader do a good job? Why or why not?
6. What transitions did the group leader use?

IV. Pronunciation Practice: Final -s as [s], [z], and [əz]

The -s ending that forms plural nouns in English can have three different pronunciations: [s], [z], and the new syllable [əz].

- When the last sound in the singular noun is voiceless (with no vibration in the throat), the -s ending will sound like [s].

  EXAMPLES:

  lips   hats   lakes

- When the last sound in the singular noun is voiced (with vibration in the throat), the -s ending will sound like [z].

  EXAMPLES:

  cars   shoes   cans

- When the last sound in the singular noun is [s], [z], [ʃ] (sh), [tʃ] (ch), [ʒ] (zh), or [ʤ] (dzh), the -s or –es ending sounds like the new syllable [əz].

  EXAMPLES:

  kiss**es**   ros**es**   dish**es**   speech**es**   garag**es**   edg**es**

ACTIVITY 1 Practice Saying Final -s like [s]

Listen and repeat the short sentences. Be sure to pronounce final -s as [s].

1. Eat the **cakes.**
2. Feed the **cats.**
3. Buy **stamps.**
4. Place the **bets.**
5. Wash the **cups.**

ACTIVITY 2 Practice Saying Final -s like [z]

Listen and repeat the short sentences. Be sure to pronounce final -s as [z].

1. Sing some **songs.**
2. Buy new **shoes.**
3. The **eggs** broke.
4. Close your **eyes.**
5. Write the **letters.**

ACTIVITY 3   Practice Saying -s or -es like the New Syllable [əz]

Listen and repeat the short sentences. Be sure to pronounce final -s or -es as the new syllable [əz].

1. I bought some **glasses.**
2. Fix the broken **dishes.**
3. **Oranges** are healthy.
4. The **watches** tell time.
5. Win the **prizes.**

ACTIVITY 4   Identify the Sound of -s

1 Listen again to the Model Discussion on pages 114–115. Circle forty-one regular plural nouns and write them in the chart. The first two appear as examples.

-s = [s] (9 words)		-s = [z] (28 words)		-s or -es = [əz] (4 words)
		penalties		
		opinions		

2 Work with a partner. Take turns pronouncing the lists of words.

ACTIVITY 5   Practice the Model Discussion

Now work in small groups. Practice reading the Model Discussion on pages 114–115 together. Be sure to pronounce the plural nouns correctly.

V. Playing with Sayings: Sayings with Final -s Pronounced [s], [z], and [əz]

ACTIVITY 1   Learn the Meanings

1 Read the following sayings. Place a checkmark (✓) next to those you heard in the Model Discussion on pages 114–115.

_____ a. **Go to pieces:** to become very upset or unable to function
I *went to pieces* when my dog died, and I stayed in bed for a week.

_____ b. **On the books:** part of the law
Laws that require the use of seat belts while driving are already *on the books.*

_____ c. **Make tracks:** to move or work quickly
We had to *make tracks* or we would miss the plane.

_____ d. **Pull some strings:** to use one's connections to important people
I hope you can *pull some strings* and get me a job where you work.

_____ e. **All ears:** listening carefully with great interest
The students were *all ears* when their teacher talked about scholarships.

2 Match the sayings with their synonyms. Then compare answers in pairs.

_____ 1. pull some strings   a. to hurry up
_____ 2. make tracks   b. to pay careful attention
_____ 3. all ears   c. part of a record
_____ 4. go to pieces   d. to use one's influence
_____ 5. on the books   e. to become very afraid and nervous

3 Circle all the regular plural nouns in the sentences in step 1 above. Write them in the chart.

-s = [s]	-s = [z]	-s or –es = [əz]

ACTIVITY 2   **Use the Sayings**

1 Complete the following sentences with your own experiences and ideas.

a. I tried to *pull some strings* for my friend when _____

b. We need to *make tracks* if we want to _____

c. I was *all ears* when _____

d. I'll *go to pieces* if _____

e. I would like to see a new law about _____ *on the books.*

2 Work in small groups. Take turns reading your sentences aloud to each other. Be sure to pronounce the plural nouns correctly.

VI. Presentation Project: Let's Discuss It!

There are thousands of laws, government regulations, and rules in every city, state, and country in the world. Your project is to participate in an eight- to ten-minute discussion about one of them. You should pretend that you are discussing the topic with no audience watching you.

STEP 1 | Choose a Topic

A Work in groups of four or five students. Look at the following list of possible discussion topics. Brainstorm additional topics and list them on your own paper.

proper clothing for women/men	underage drinking
bullfighting	having children
dogs in restaurants	car thefts
smoking cigarettes	wearing motorcycle helmets
cheating on exams	cell phone use

B As a group, select the three topics that interest everyone the most.

C Working by yourself, go online or use the library to find some information about the three topics your group selected. Prepare to discuss the advantages and disadvantages of each topic for your group discussion.

D Meet again as a group. Review the advantages and disadvantages of each topic and select one for your group's discussion.

EXAMPLE:

Student A: *Having children isn't a good topic because there's no law against it and no penalties. There's not much to discuss.*

Student B: *That's not true. In China, families are allowed to have only one child.*

Student C: *Really? Well, should that be our discussion topic?*

STEP 2 | Plan for Your Discussion

A Choose a group leader.

B Read the steps your discussion should follow.

Introduction
1. Group leader introduces the topic.
2. Group leader describes how the discussion will be organized.

Describe the Law or Rule
Include this information:
- What is the law or rule?
- When was it passed?
- How does it affect people?

Describe Reasons for the Law
- Describe penalties for breaking the law
- Share opinions about the law

Conclusion
1. Group leader brings the discussion to a close after eight to ten minutes.
2. Group leader thanks the participants.

C Read the Useful Language expressions you can use during the discussion. Place a checkmark (✓) next to the expressions you like best.

> **USEFUL LANGUAGE: PROVIDING FEEDBACK AND REINFORCEMENT**
>
> _____ That's important to know, [name of person].
>
> _____ That's very interesting, [name of person].
>
> _____ Good point, [name of person].
>
> _____ Thanks for sharing that, [name of person].

> **USEFUL LANGUAGE: ADDING INFORMATION**
>
> _____ I'd like to add to what [name of person] said about . . .
>
> _____ Here's what I found out . . .
>
> _____ Yes, I also read that . . .

D Research your group's topic on your own. Be prepared to participate in a group discussion about it in class on the scheduled date.

E Select a saying from pages 118–119 to include during the discussion. Write it here:

_____

STEP 3 | Prepare Discussion Note Cards

A. Group Member Note Cards

1 Prepare at least one note card for each part of the discussion. Label the cards:

- Description of the Law
- Reasons for the Law
- Penalties for Breaking the Law
- My Opinion

2 Add important details from your research notes.

3 Number your cards.

4 Add Useful Language expressions from this page and a saying from pages 118–119 to your notes.

B. Group Leader Note Cards

1 Prepare the following note cards.

- Introduction + preview
- Transition to Part 1: Description of the Law
- Transition to Part 2: Reasons for the Law
- Transition to Part 3: Penalties for Breaking the Law
- Transition to Part 4: Asking Group Members for Their Opinions
- Conclusion

2 Add your opener, transitions, and conclusion.

3 Number your cards.

4 Read the Useful Language expressions you can use to prepare transitions. Place a checkmark (✓) next to the expressions you like best.

> ### USEFUL LANGUAGE: GROUP LEADER TRANSITIONS
> _____ Let's begin by . . . Who wants to go first?
>
> _____ We now know details about (the law). Let's now talk about . . .
>
> _____ You have all given good reasons for (the law). Next we'll discuss . . .
>
> _____ We've discussed (the law). Now it's time to . . .

STEP 4 | Review Your Notes

A Read your notes aloud several times to become familiar with them.

B Complete the discussion preparation checklist. Is there anything you want to change or add to your note cards before the scheduled discussion?

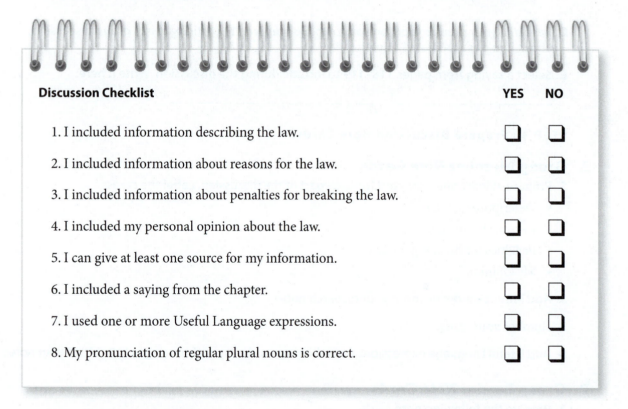

Discussion Checklist	YES	NO
1. I included information describing the law.	☐	☐
2. I included information about reasons for the law.	☐	☐
3. I included information about penalties for breaking the law.	☐	☐
4. I included my personal opinion about the law.	☐	☐
5. I can give at least one source for my information.	☐	☐
6. I included a saying from the chapter.	☐	☐
7. I used one or more Useful Language expressions.	☐	☐
8. My pronunciation of regular plural nouns is correct.	☐	☐

C Your teacher and/or your classmates may evaluate your participation in the discussion. Study the form on page 148 so you know how you will be evaluated. You may use the items on the form to make final changes to your notes.

STEP 5 | Participate in the Group Discussion

A Relax, take a deep breath, and join in the discussion.

B Listen to your audience's applause.

CHAPTER 10

TELL ME A STORY

The ability to tell a story well is a wonderful skill to have. Listeners remember a good story much longer then they remember other types of presentations. You will delight audiences of all ages by telling them a story!

CHAPTER CHALLENGE Your challenge in this final chapter is to learn and apply the basic elements of storytelling. By the time you complete this chapter, you will be able to:

- identify ways to use your voice to make story characters seem real
- identify gestures and facial expressions to use to make a story come alive
- organize and develop the plot of a story from beginning to end
- plan, prepare, and present a fable (a traditional story that teaches a lesson)

I. Making Your Story Come Alive

Follow these tips to get and keep your listeners' interest.

1. **Change your voice to indicate different characters.**

   EXAMPLES:
   - Use a high-pitched voice for a young or small character (a child, a mouse, etc.)
   - Use a low, deep voice for a larger or older character (a bear; a big, strong man, etc.)

2. **Look in different directions to indicate different characters.**

   EXAMPLES:
   - Always look to the right when you say (in a low, deep voice), "The bear said . . ."
   - Always look to the left when you say (in a high, squeaky voice), "The mouse cried . . ."

3. **Perform the actions described in the written story.**

   EXAMPLES:
   - If the text says, "The bear sneezed," you could say "ah-ah-chooo!" at that point in the story.
   - If it says, "The princess covered her ears," you can cover your ears.

4. **Use the facial expressions described in the story.**

   EXAMPLES:
   - If the text says, "The girl frowned," you should frown, too.
   - If it says, "He was surprised," you should open your eyes wide and look surprised.

5. **Ask the audience to participate.**

   EXAMPLE:
   - If the story says, "Everyone clapped and cheered," ask the audience to clap their hands and yell "Hurray, hurray."

6. **Show actual objects mentioned in the story.**

   EXAMPLES:
   - If the story says, "The cook rang a bell," bring a bell to class and ring it.
   - If it says, "The farmer started to dig a hole with a small shovel," bring a shovel to class and pretend to dig.

ACTIVITY 1 Make the Story Come Alive

1 Work in small groups. Read the following lines from actual fables. Think about ways to make the characters come alive. Write your ideas in the spaces. The first item is done for you as an example.

a. The lamb cried in a worried tone of voice, "I wasn't even born then."
   (*Source:* "The Wolf and the Lamb")

   <u>look very worried; speak in a high voice; make the sound "baaa, baaa"</u>

b. The mouse begged the lion, "Please sir, don't eat me." (*Source:* "The Lion and the Mouse")

   _____

c. One by one, the father put a stick into his sons' hands and ordered them, "Now break it into pieces." (*Source*: "The Father and His Sons")

_____

d. A traveler saw his dog standing at the door, stretching. He asked him in an angry way, "Why do you stand there doing nothing?" (*Source*: "The Traveler and His Dog")

_____

e. A very hungry fox tried to reach a bunch of grapes hanging high up on a vine. He jumped as high as he could but still couldn't reach them. (*Source*: "The Fox and the Grapes")

_____

f. Once there was a boy watching the village sheep. He wanted some attention so he called loudly, "Wolf! Wolf! Help! A wolf is attacking the sheep!" (*Source*: "The Boy Who Cried Wolf")

_____

g. One winter day a farmer found a snake frozen with cold. He picked it up and placed it under his jacket to warm up. (*Source*: "The Farmer and the Snake")

_____

h. The fox turned around, looked at the goat, and laughed at him. He said, "You are a foolish old goat." (*Source*: "The Fox and the Goat")

_____

i. Patty was going to market to sell her milk. She carried her milk in a pail on her head. (*Source*: "The Milkmaid and Her Pail")

_____

j. The stork begged the farmer, "Please let me go free. Look at my feathers; they are not like those of a Crane." (*Source*: "The Stork and the Cranes")

_____

2 Take turns reading the sentences. Be sure to:

1. change your voice to indicate different characters
2. use any facial expressions described
3. perform any actions described

In a progressive story, one person in a group starts a story and the other group members take turns adding parts until the story is complete.

1 Work in groups of four. Take turns reading the parts of the model progressive story aloud. Pay attention to how the four speakers begin, continue, and end the story.

MODEL PROGRESSIVE STORY: "How We Spent a Sunday"

Speaker A: I had a surprise phone call from my cousin Pedro yesterday. He invited me and three friends to go for a ride in his new car. We decided to drive to the forest for a picnic. He came to pick us up and then all five of us got into his small car and drove off. On the way Pedro was driving really fast. I told him to slow down, but he wouldn't listen. All of a sudden we saw a police car behind us. The officer turned on his flashing lights and . . .

Speaker B: The police officer started chasing us. I was sure we were going to get a speeding ticket. Well, the officer pulled us over to the side of the road, and that's exactly what happened. He started to write Pedro a ticket for speeding. All of a sudden he saw our bumper sticker that said "Colombia." He got a really angry look on his face and . . .

Speaker C: He made all five of us get out of the car, and he started to search it. He opened the trunk and saw two canvas bags in there. He asked us what was in the bags. Pedro told him they were full of coffee from Colombia. His dad owns a large coffee company there, and he had just returned from a trip to Colombia to visit our family. Of course the policeman didn't believe him. Pedro tried to convince him he was telling the truth, but the officer wouldn't listen.

Speaker D: After that the officer made us drive to the police station. When we got there, another policeman took the coffee away. We waited there for three hours while they tested the coffee. Finally they came back and said it was real. Then they invited us to share a cake they had in the kitchen of the police station. They asked if we would make the coffee. We all had a party! Then they said they were sorry and let us go. We never did get a speeding ticket. Pedro made me promise not to tell my parents what happened!

---

2 Discuss these questions with your group members.

a. Who are the people in the story?

b. What did they plan to do?

c. How does Speaker A begin telling the action in the story?

d. What does Speaker B do to continue the story?

e. What new details does Speaker B make up?

f. How does Speaker C continue describing what happened?

g. How does Speaker D contribute to the story?

ACTIVITY 3   Create a Progressive Story

1 Work with a new group of four classmates. Read the guidelines for organizing a progressive story.

Speaker A: Introduces the Story
- Tells who the people in the story are
- Describes their plans
- Starts telling the action in the story

Speaker B: Continues the Story
- Describes the next thing that happens
- Makes up details

Speaker C: Continues the Story
- Continues describing what happened
- Continues making up details

Speaker D: Concludes the Story
- Provides final details about what happened
- Tells how the story ends

2 Working with your group, create your own progressive story. Choose one of the following openers to begin your story or create one of your own.

> A good friend of mine called yesterday and . . .
> On my way to class the other day . . .
> I had the greatest weekend. I . . .
> I had a terrible argument with my . . .
> Last night I had a really weird dream. I dreamt that . . .

3 Each group member should speak for about one minute.

4 Share your progressive story with the class.

II. Presentation Preview

Your goal in this section is to choose a fable and prepare a speech about it with many colorful details.

ACTIVITY 1 Listen to a Model Fable

Listen to Flavia tell the well-known fable "The Tortoise and the Hare." Notice the way she changes her voice to indicate the different characters.

MODEL STORY: A Fabulous Fable

INTRODUCTION

Have you ever felt that you couldn't do something because it was too hard? Have you ever stopped working toward a goal because you thought it would take too long to finish? I think we've all avoided certain situations because we thought we would fail at them. Well, after you hear my fable, I hope you won't let a difficult situation discourage you anymore.

Today, I'm going to tell you the story of the Tortoise and the Hare.

And here are the stars of my story!

BODY

Once upon a time, there was a very fast Hare, who bragged that he could run faster than anyone. For a long time Tortoise, who was a very slow animal, *held his tongue* and never said a word. Finally, however, he became tired of hearing Hare brag about how fast he was, and he said [**Flavia looks to the left**], "Who do you think you are? I'm sure someone could beat you!" Hare laughed [**Flavia imitates a laugh: "Ha ha ha!"**] and said [**Flavia looks to the right**], "Who? Do **you** want to try? Nobody in the whole world can beat **me**!" Tortoise shrugged his shoulders. [**Flavia shrugs her shoulders**]. He **was** sure he would lose but decided to try anyhow. The race began and immediately. Hare ran fast ahead. He *had high hopes* of winning. He looked back at Tortoise and called [**Flavia pretends to look behind her**], "How do you expect to win? You are soooooooo slow." Soon Tortoise was out of sight. Hare was so confident that he stopped to take a nap. He fell asleep happily and told himself [**Flavia looks toward the right**], "I have plenty of time to sleep."

* Kept quiet

* Expected a good result

While Hare slept, Tortoise kept on walking. He walked and walked until he was almost at the finish line. All the animals in the forest clapped and cheered. [**Flavia tells the audience to clap and yell "Hurray, hurray!"**] The noise woke up Hare. He yawned [**Flavia opens her mouth wide and yawns loudly**] and stretched his arms over his head [**Flavia stretches her arms over her head**], thinking that Tortoise was far behind him. But then he saw Tortoise crossing the finish line! Hare began to run again, but it was too late. Tortoise had already won!

In the end, Hare understood his mistake. He told himself, "I was too confident. Tortoise beat me because he never stopped walking toward his goal. Slow and steady wins the race every time!"

Transition — This fable teaches us not to be too confident. But it also teaches another important lesson.

Explanation of Lesson — Don't give up even if you are slow or not as good at something as someone else. If you keep going, little by little you will succeed.

Transition — Let me give you an example from my own life.

Real-Life Example — Sometimes I feel that English is too hard and I will never be able to speak it perfectly. Then I think about Tortoise. He kept moving ahead to reach his goal. I know that if I keep practicing, I will improve a little each day. I already speak much better than I did at first. Maybe one day I will speak as well as our teacher!

CONCLUSION Repeat the Lesson — So, I hope you take my advice and *hang in there*.* Remember, slow and steady wins the race!

Don't give up

Thank the Audience — I hope you enjoyed my fable speech. Thank you so much for listening.

ACTIVITY 2 **Fill in the Blanks**

1 Listen to Flavia's Fabulous Fable speech again. Fill in the blanks with the correct words from her speech.

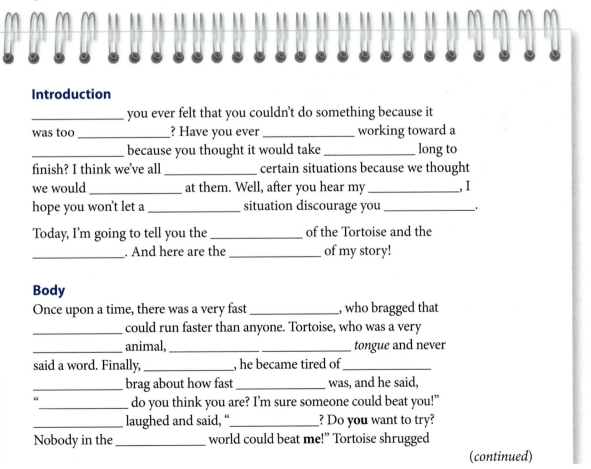

Introduction

_____ you ever felt that you couldn't do something because it was too _____? Have you ever _____ working toward a _____ because you thought it would take _____ long to finish? I think we've all _____ certain situations because we thought we would _____ at them. Well, after you hear my _____, I hope you won't let a _____ situation discourage you _____.

Today, I'm going to tell you the _____ of the Tortoise and the _____. And here are the _____ of my story!

Body

Once upon a time, there was a very fast _____, who bragged that _____ could run faster than anyone. Tortoise, who was a very _____ animal, _____ _____ *tongue* and never said a word. Finally, _____, he became tired of _____ _____ brag about how fast _____ was, and he said, "_____ do you think you are? I'm sure someone could beat you!" _____ laughed and said, "_____? Do **you** want to try? Nobody in the _____ world could beat **me**!" Tortoise shrugged

(*continued*)

(*Continued*)

_____ shoulders. _____ was sure _____ would lose but decided to try _____. The race began and immediately. Hare ran fast ahead. He _____ _____ _____ of winning. He looked back at Tortoise and called, "_____ do you expect to win? You are sooooooo slow." Soon Tortoise was out of sight. Hare was so confident that _____ stopped to take a nap. He fell asleep _____ and told _____, "I _____ plenty of time to sleep."

While _____ slept, Tortoise kept on walking. _____ walked and walked until _____ was almost at the finish line. All the animals in the forest clapped and cheered. The noise woke up _____. _____ yawned and stretched _____ arms over _____ _____, thinking that Tortoise was far behind _____. But then _____ saw Tortoise crossing the finish line! _____ began to run again, but it was too late. Tortoise _____ already won!

In the end, _____ understood _____ mistake. He told _____, "I was too overconfident. Tortoise beat me because he never stopped walking toward _____ goal. Slow and steady wins the race every time!"

Transition

This fable teaches us not to be too confident. But it also teaches another important lesson.

Explanation of Lesson

Don't give up even if you are slow or not as good at something as someone else. If you keep going, little by little you will succeed.

Transition

Let me give you an example from my own life.

Real-Life Example

Sometimes I feel that English is too _____ and I will never be able to speak it perfectly. Then I think about Tortoise. _____ kept moving _____ to reach _____ goal. I know that if I keep practicing, I will improve a little each day. I already speak much better than I did at first. Maybe one day I will speak as well as our teacher!

Conclusion

Repeat the Lesson

So, I hope you take my advice and _____ *in* _____ Remember, slow and steady wins the race!

Thank the Audience

I _____ you enjoyed my fable speech. Thank you so much for listening.

2 Compare your answers with a partner's.

ACTIVITY 3 **Model Speech Discussion**

Discuss these questions in small groups.

1. Did Flavia's introduction get your attention? How?
2. How did Flavia indicate the different characters in her story?
3. How did she get the audience to participate?
4. Did Flavia perform the actions described in the story? Which ones?
5. What speech aids did Flavia use? Which others could she have used?
6. What lesson did the story teach? How did Flavia explain it?
7. What real-life example did Flavia give to illustrate the fable?
8. Have you had any experiences proving the lesson, "Slow and steady wins the race"? What were they?

III. Pronunciation Practice: [h]

The sound [h] can be confusing for many learners of English. If you omit [h], *hat* sounds like *at*; if you substitute [f] or [ʃ], *Hugh* sounds like *few* and *heat* sounds like *sheet*.

To pronounce [h], relax your throat and tongue. Gently let out a puff of air as if you were sighing.

ACTIVITY 1 **Word Practice**

Listen and repeat the following words. Focus on letting out a puff of air as you say [h].

[h] at the Beginning of Words	[h] in the Middle of Words
1. he	6. ahead
2. who	7. behind
3. here	8. behave
4. heat	9. inhale
5. home	10. unhappy

ACTIVITY 2 **Sentence Practice**

Listen and repeat the following sentences.

1. **Hurry** up!
2. What **happened**?
3. **How have** you been?
4. **Henry hit** a **home** run.
5. **Helen has** brown **hair**.

PRONUNCIATION TIPS

- The *sound* [h] does not occur at the ends of words. (The *letter* "h" at the end of words is silent).
- The "wh" in the words *who, whom, whose, and whole* is pronounced [h].

🎧 **1** Listen to Flavia's speech on pages 129 and 130 again. Circle the words pronounced with [h].

2 Complete the chart with words from Flavia's speech.

[h] at the Beginning of Words		[h] in the Middle of Words

3 Work with a partner. Take turns pronouncing the words aloud several times.

4 Take turns reading Flavia's fable aloud. Be sure you pronounce [h] with a puff of air.

IV. Playing with Sayings: Sayings with [h]

ACTIVITY 1 Learn the Meaning

1 Read the following sayings. Place a checkmark (√) next to those you heard in the Model Story.

_____ a. **Hang in there:** don't give up

Svetlana almost dropped her difficult chemistry class. In the end she *hung in there* and earned a B+!

_____ b. **To hold one's tongue:** to keep quiet

I *held my tongue* and didn't tell anyone the secret.

_____ c. **Hit the nail on the head:** to get the answer exactly right

Helen *hit the nail on the head* and won the game.

_____ d. **To have high hopes:** to hope for a good result

Hank *had high hopes* that he would win the prize.

_____ e. **Hold your horses:** wait; be patient

Don't buy the first house you see; *hold your horses* and shop around.

2 Circle the [h] sounds in the sayings in Activity 1. Say each saying aloud several times.

ACTIVITY 2 Use the Sayings

1 **Work in small groups. Unscramble the sayings and write them in the correct order.**

a. I (*hopes high have*) _____ that I will get an A in all my classes.

b. He (*nail hit the head on the*) _____ when he suggested a perfect
solution to the problem.

c. My dad told me to (*my horses hold*) _____ when I wanted to buy the
first car I saw.

d. The teacher told the student to (*his tongue hold*) _____ and to stop
interrupting his classmates.

e. When my friend wanted to drop out of school, I told her (*hang there in*)
" _____ ."

ACTIVITY 3 Use the Sayings in Questions and Answers

1 **Work in pairs. Take turns asking the questions and completing the answers. Try to use words
pronounced with [h] in your answers.**

EXAMPLES:

A: Who has *high hopes?*

B: I have *high hopes* that my <u>husband Henry and I will win the lottery</u>.

A: Have you ever told anyone to *hold her horses*?
B: I told my <u>friend Helen</u> to *hold her horses* and not <u>hurry to get married</u>.

a. A: Have you ever been told to *hang in there?*

 B: My _____ told me to *hang in there* when _____.

b. A: Have you ever told anyone to *hold his tongue?*

 B: I told my _____ to hold his tongue when_____.

c. A: Who has *high hopes?*

 B: _____ has *high hopes* that_____.

d. A: Have you ever *hit the nail on the head?*

 B: I *hit the nail on the head* when _____.

e. A: Have you ever told anyone to *hold her horses?*

 B: I told _____ to *hold her horses* and not _____.

2 **Take turns reading your sentences aloud to each other. Be sure to pronounce [h] with
a puff of air.**

V. Presentation Project: The Fabulous Fable

Your project is to prepare and present a fable. You should speak for two to three minutes. Get ready to become a storyteller!

STEP 1 | Choose a Fable

A There are hundreds of fables to choose from. Find one you like in the children's section of a library or bookstore or online (use the search term "fables").

B Read the story many times to become very familiar with it.

C Tell the story to at least five friends and family members before planning your speech.

STEP 2 | Plan Your Speech

A Read the guidelines for organizing your Fabulous Fable speech.

Introduction
1. Include an attention-getting opener.
2. Tell the name of your fable.

Body
1. Tell the story:
   - Change your voice and look in different directions to indicate different characters.
   - Use any facial expressions described.
   - Perform any actions described.
2. Tell the lesson of the fable.
3. Add a transition to the explanation of the fable.
4. Explain the lesson that the fable teaches.
5. Add a transition to your real-life example.
6. Relate the fable to your own life.

Conclusion
1. Repeat the lesson taught by the fable.
2. Thank your audience for listening.

B Read the Useful Language expressions you can use to begin telling the story. Place a checkmark (✓) next to the expressions you like best.

> **USEFUL LANGUAGE: BEGINNING A STORY**
>
> _____ Once upon a time . . .
>
> _____ Long ago, when animals could talk, there was . . .
>
> _____ Once, long before we were born, . . .

C Include at least one speech aid.

D Select a saying from page 132 to include in your speech. Write it here:_____.

E Complete the following outline with notes for your speech.

The Fabulous Fable: Speech Preparation Outline

Name of Fable: _____

Introduction
Attention Getter

_____

_____

_____

Name of Fable

_____

Body
The Story

_____

_____

_____

_____

_____

_____

The Lesson of the Fable

_____

_____

Transition _____

Meaning of the Lesson _____

Transition _____

(continued)

(Continued)

Real-Life Example

_____

_____

_____

Conclusion
Repeat the Lesson

_____

_____

Thank the Audience

_____

_____

STEP 3 | Prepare Note Cards

A Use the guidelines in Step 2 to prepare note cards for your speech. Label the cards:

- Attention Getter + Name of Fable
- The Story + Lesson of the Fable
- Transition + Meaning of Lesson
- Transition + Real-Life Example
- Conclusion

B Fill in details from your outline. Use as many cards as you need.

C Add the saying you selected to your notes.

D Number your cards.

STEP 4 | Practice Your Speech

A Practice your speech in front of a mirror using your note cards. Record it and listen to it at least once. Be sure it is two to three minutes long.

B Complete the Speech Checklist on the next page. Is there anything you want to change or improve before you present your speech in class?

Speech Checklist

	YES	NO
1. I included an introduction and stated the name of the fable.	❏	❏
2. I changed my voice and looked in different directions to indicate different characters.	❏	❏
3. I performed the actions and used facial expressions described in the story.	❏	❏
4. I involved the audience and used actual objects mentioned in the story.	❏	❏
5. I told the lesson of the fable and explained its meaning.	❏	❏
6. I included a real-life example.	❏	❏
7. I repeated the lesson and thanked the audience.	❏	❏
8. I included transitions.	❏	❏
9. I included a saying from the chapter.	❏	❏
10. I included a speech aid.	❏	❏
11. My pronunciation of [h] is clear.	❏	❏
12. My speech is 2 to 3 minutes long.	❏	❏

C Practice again with your note cards and speech aid.

D Your teacher and/or your classmates may evaluate your speech. Study the form on page 150 so you know how you will be evaluated. You may use the items on the form to make final changes to your speech.

STEP 5 | Present Your Speech

A Relax, take a deep breath, and present your fable.

B Listen to your audience's applause!

About Me! Brainstorming Balloons (Page 7)

SPEAKER: _____   DATE: _____

EVALUATOR: _____

DELIVERY	RATING			COMMENTS
POSTURE	1	2	3	_____
EYE CONTACT	1	2	3	_____
VOLUME OF VOICE	1	2	3	_____
ENTHUSIASM	1	2	3	_____
SPOKE WITHIN TIME LIMIT	1	2	3	_____

ADDITIONAL COMMENTS ABOUT DELIVERY

_____

_____

_____

CONTENT	RATING			COMMENTS
INTRODUCTION	1	2	3	_____
BACKGROUND/EARLY CHILDHOOD	1	2	3	_____
FAMILY	1	2	3	_____
CURRENT ACTIVITIES	1	2	3	_____
HOBBIES/SPECIAL INTERESTS	1	2	3	_____
FUTURE PLANS	1	2	3	_____
SUMMARY SENTENCE	1	2	3	_____
THANKED AUDIENCE	1	2	3	_____
SAYING FROM CHAPTER	1	2	3	_____
USEFUL LANGUAGE	1	2	3	_____

ADDITIONAL COMMENTS ABOUT CONTENT

_____

_____

_____

RATING KEY

1 = NEEDS IMPROVEMENT/PRACTICE   2 = GOOD   3 = EXCELLENT

About Me! Photo Story (Page 12)

SPEAKER: _____   DATE: _____

EVALUATOR: _____

DELIVERY	RATING			COMMENTS
POSTURE	1	2	3	_____
EYE CONTACT	1	2	3	_____
VOLUME OF VOICE	1	2	3	_____
ENTHUSIASM	1	2	3	_____
SPOKE WITHIN TIME LIMIT	1	2	3	_____

ADDITIONAL COMMENTS ABOUT DELIVERY

_____

_____

_____

CONTENT	RATING			COMMENTS
INTRODUCTION	1	2	3	_____
DETAILS ABOUT PAST	1	2	3	_____
DETAILS ABOUT PRESENT	1	2	3	_____
DETAILS ABOUT FUTURE	1	2	3	_____
SUMMARY SENTENCE	1	2	3	_____
THANKED AUDIENCE	1	2	3	_____
SAYING FROM CHAPTER	1	2	3	_____
USEFUL LANGUAGE	1	2	3	_____

ADDITIONAL COMMENTS ABOUT CONTENT

_____

_____

_____

RATING KEY

1 = NEEDS IMPROVEMENT/PRACTICE   2 = GOOD   3 = EXCELLENT

CHAPTER 2

Meaningful Object (Page 22)

SPEAKER: _____   DATE: _____

EVALUATOR: _____

DELIVERY	RATING			COMMENTS
POSTURE/GESTURES	1	2	3	_____
EYE CONTACT	1	2	3	_____
VOLUME OF VOICE	1	2	3	_____
ENTHUSIASM	1	2	3	_____
SPOKE WITHIN TIME LIMIT	1	2	3	_____

ADDITIONAL COMMENTS ABOUT DELIVERY

_____
_____
_____

CONTENT	RATING			COMMENTS
CHOICE OF OBJECT	1	2	3	_____
INTRODUCTION	1	2	3	_____
FACTS ABOUT OBJECT	1	2	3	_____
FEELINGS ABOUT OBJECT	1	2	3	_____
CONCLUSION	1	2	3	_____
THANKED AUDIENCE	1	2	3	_____
SAYING FROM CHAPTER	1	2	3	_____
USEFUL LANGUAGE	1	2	3	_____

ADDITIONAL COMMENTS ABOUT CONTENT

_____
_____
_____
_____

RATING KEY

1 = NEEDS IMPROVEMENT/PRACTICE   2 = GOOD   3 = EXCELLENT

CHAPTER 3

Worst Fear (Page 35)

SPEAKER: _____ DATE: _____

EVALUATOR: _____

DELIVERY	RATING			COMMENTS
POSTURE/GESTURES	1	2	3	_____
EYE CONTACT	1	2	3	_____
VOLUME OF VOICE	1	2	3	_____
ENTHUSIASM	1	2	3	_____
SPOKE WITHIN TIME LIMIT	1	2	3	_____

ADDITIONAL COMMENTS ABOUT DELIVERY

_____

_____

_____

CONTENT	RATING			COMMENTS
CHOICE OF TOPIC	1	2	3	_____
ATTENTION GETTER	1	2	3	_____
PREVIEW	1	2	3	_____
DETAILS	1	2	3	_____
SPEECH AIDS	1	2	3	_____
CONCLUSION	1	2	3	_____
THANKED AUDIENCE	1	2	3	_____
SAYING FROM CHAPTER	1	2	3	_____
USEFUL LANGUAGE	1	2	3	_____

ADDITIONAL COMMENTS ABOUT CONTENT

_____

_____

_____

_____

RATING KEY

1 = NEEDS IMPROVEMENT/PRACTICE   2 = GOOD   3 = EXCELLENT

CHAPTER 4

Report on an Interview (Page 52)

SPEAKER: _____   DATE: _____

EVALUATOR: _____

DELIVERY	RATING			COMMENTS
POSTURE/GESTURES	1	2	3	_____
EYE CONTACT	1	2	3	_____
VOLUME OF VOICE	1	2	3	_____
ENTHUSIASM	1	2	3	_____
SPOKE WITHIN TIME LIMIT	1	2	3	_____

ADDITIONAL COMMENTS ABOUT DELIVERY

_____

_____

_____

CONTENT	RATING			COMMENTS
CHOICE OF TOPIC	1	2	3	_____
ATTENTION GETTER	1	2	3	_____
INFO ABOUT INTERVIEWEE	1	2	3	_____
DETAILS	1	2	3	_____
USE OF RESTATEMENTS	1	2	3	_____
RHETORICAL QUESTIONS	1	2	3	_____
SPEECH AIDS	1	2	3	_____
FINAL STATEMENT(S)	1	2	3	_____
THANKED AUDIENCE	1	2	3	_____
SAYING FROM CHAPTER	1	2	3	_____
USEFUL LANGUAGE	1	2	3	_____

ADDITIONAL COMMENTS ABOUT CONTENT

_____

_____

_____

RATING KEY

1 = NEEDS IMPROVEMENT/PRACTICE   2 = GOOD   3 = EXCELLENT

CHAPTER 5

Explain It! (Page 65)

SPEAKER: _____   DATE: _____

EVALUATOR: _____

DELIVERY	RATING			COMMENTS
POSTURE/GESTURES	1	2	3	_____
EYE CONTACT	1	2	3	_____
VOLUME OF VOICE	1	2	3	_____
ENTHUSIASM	1	2	3	_____
SPOKE WITHIN TIME LIMIT	1	2	3	_____

ADDITIONAL COMMENTS ABOUT DELIVERY

_____

_____

_____

CONTENT	RATING			COMMENTS
CHOICE OF TOPIC	1	2	3	_____
ATTENTION GETTER	1	2	3	_____
STATEMENT OF PROBLEM	1	2	3	_____
PREVIEW	1	2	3	_____
CAUSES OF PROBLEM	1	2	3	_____
SOLUTIONS TO PROBLEM	1	2	3	_____
TRANSITIONS	1	2	3	_____
SPEECH AIDS	1	2	3	_____
SUMMARY	1	2	3	_____
FINAL REMARKS	1	2	3	_____
SAYING FROM CHAPTER	1	2	3	_____
USEFUL LANGUAGE	1	2	3	_____

ADDITIONAL COMMENTS ABOUT CONTENT

_____

_____

_____

RATING KEY

1 = NEEDS IMPROVEMENT/PRACTICE   2 = GOOD   3 = EXCELLENT

CHAPTER 6

Demonstrate It! (Page 80)

SPEAKER: _____   DATE: _____

EVALUATOR: _____

DELIVERY	RATING			COMMENTS
POSTURE/GESTURES	1	2	3	_____
EYE CONTACT	1	2	3	_____
VOLUME OF VOICE	1	2	3	_____
ENTHUSIASM	1	2	3	_____
SPOKE WITHIN TIME LIMIT	1	2	3	_____

ADDITIONAL COMMENTS ABOUT DELIVERY

_____

_____

_____

CONTENT	RATING			COMMENTS
CHOICE OF TOPIC	1	2	3	_____
ATTENTION GETTER	1	2	3	_____
STATEMENT OF TOPIC	1	2	3	_____
PREVIEW	1	2	3	_____
CLEAR STEP-BY-STEP DIRECTIONS	1	2	3	_____
DIFFICULT STEPS EMPHASIZED	1	2	3	_____
TRANSITIONS	1	2	3	_____
SPEECH AIDS	1	2	3	_____
AUDIENCE ENCOURAGEMENT	1	2	3	_____
FINAL REMARKS	1	2	3	_____
SAYING FROM CHAPTER	1	2	3	_____
USEFUL LANGUAGE	1	2	3	_____

ADDITIONAL COMMENTS ABOUT CONTENT

_____

_____

_____

RATING KEY

1 = NEEDS IMPROVEMENT/PRACTICE   2 = GOOD   3 = EXCELLENT

CHAPTER 7

A Culture Conflict (Page 93)

SPEAKER: _____   DATE: _____

EVALUATOR: _____

DELIVERY	RATING			COMMENTS
POSTURE/GESTURES	1	2	3	_____
EYE CONTACT	1	2	3	_____
VOLUME OF VOICE	1	2	3	_____
ENTHUSIASM	1	2	3	_____
SPOKE WITHIN TIME LIMIT	1	2	3	_____

ADDITIONAL COMMENTS ABOUT DELIVERY

_____

_____

_____

CONTENT	RATING			COMMENTS
CHOICE OF TOPIC	1	2	3	_____
INTRODUCTION	1	2	3	_____
PREVIEW	1	2	3	_____
DETAILS	1	2	3	_____
SPEECH AIDS	1	2	3	_____
FINAL STATEMENTS	1	2	3	_____
THANKED AUDIENCE	1	2	3	_____
SAYING FROM CHAPTER	1	2	3	_____
USEFUL LANGUAGE	1	2	3	_____

ADDITIONAL COMMENTS ABOUT CONTENT

_____

_____

_____

_____

RATING KEY

1 = NEEDS IMPROVEMENT/PRACTICE   2 = GOOD   3 = EXCELLENT

CHAPTER 8

Convince Me! (Page 106)

SPEAKER: _____   DATE: _____

EVALUATOR: _____

DELIVERY	RATING			COMMENTS
POSTURE/GESTURES	1	2	3	_____
EYE CONTACT	1	2	3	_____
VOLUME OF VOICE	1	2	3	_____
ENTHUSIASM	1	2	3	_____
SPOKE WITHIN TIME LIMIT	1	2	3	_____

ADDITIONAL COMMENTS ABOUT DELIVERY

_____

_____

_____

_____

CONTENT	RATING			COMMENTS
CHOICE OF TOPIC	1	2	3	_____
ATTENTION STEP	1	2	3	_____
NEED STEP	1	2	3	_____
SATISFACTION STEP	1	2	3	_____
VISUALIZATION STEP	1	2	3	_____
ACTION STEP	1	2	3	_____
SPEECH AIDS	1	2	3	_____
SAYING FROM CHAPTER	1	2	3	_____
USEFUL LANGUAGE	1	2	3	_____

ADDITIONAL COMMENTS ABOUT CONTENT

_____

_____

_____

_____

RATING KEY

1 = NEEDS IMPROVEMENT/PRACTICE   2 = GOOD   3 = EXCELLENT

Let's Discuss It! (Page 119)
Individual Group Member Evaluation

SPEAKER: _____   TOPIC: _____

EVALUATOR: _____   DATE: _____

PREPARATION	RATING			COMMENTS
EVIDENCE OF PLANNING	1	2	3	_____
EVIDENCE OF RESEARCH	1	2	3	_____

PARTICIPATION				
STAYED ON TRACK	1	2	3	_____
ENTHUSIASM	1	2	3	_____
SUFFICIENT CONTRIBUTIONS	1	2	3	_____

VALUE OF CONTRIBUTIONS				
DESCRIPTION OF LAW	1	2	3	_____
REASONS FOR LAW	1	2	3	_____
PENALTIES FOR BREAKING LAW	1	2	3	_____
PERSONAL OPINIONS	1	2	3	_____
SOURCES CITED	1	2	3	_____
SAYING FROM CHAPTER	1	2	3	_____
USEFUL LANGUAGE	1	2	3	_____

ADDITIONAL COMMENTS

_____

_____

_____

_____

_____

_____

RATING KEY

1 = NEEDS IMPROVEMENT/PRACTICE   2 = GOOD   3 = EXCELLENT

Let's Discuss It! (Page 119)
Group Leader Evaluation

LEADER: _____   TOPIC: _____

EVALUATOR: _____   DATE: _____

EFFECTIVENESS	RATING			COMMENTS
INTRODUCTION OF TOPIC	1	2	3	_____
INTRODUCTION OF PARTICIPANTS	1	2	3	_____
KEPT GROUP ORGANIZED	1	2	3	_____
KEPT GROUP WITHIN TIME LIMIT	1	2	3	_____
KNOWLEDGE OF TOPIC	1	2	3	_____
ENCOURAGED PARTICIPATION	1	2	3	_____
TRANSITIONS	1	2	3	_____
CONCLUSION	1	2	3	_____
USEFUL LANGUAGE	1	2	3	_____

ADDITIONAL COMMENTS

_____

_____

_____

_____

_____

RATING KEY

1 = NEEDS IMPROVEMENT/PRACTICE   2 = GOOD   3 = EXCELLENT

CHAPTER 10

The Fabulous Fable (Page 134)

SPEAKER: _____   DATE: _____

EVALUATOR: _____

DELIVERY	RATING			COMMENTS
POSTURE/GESTURES	1	2	3	_____
EYE CONTACT	1	2	3	_____
USE OF VOICE	1	2	3	_____
FACIAL EXPRESSIONS	1	2	3	_____
SPOKE WITHIN TIME LIMIT	1	2	3	_____

ADDITIONAL COMMENTS ABOUT DELIVERY

_____

_____

_____

CONTENT	RATING			COMMENTS
CHOICE OF TOPIC	1	2	3	_____
INTRODUCTION	1	2	3	_____
TELLING OF FABLE	1	2	3	_____
AUDIENCE INVOLVEMENT	1	2	3	_____
MEANING OF LESSON	1	2	3	_____
REAL-LIFE EXAMPLE	1	2	3	_____
TRANSITIONS	1	2	3	_____
SPEECH AIDS	1	2	3	_____
CONCLUSION	1	2	3	_____
SAYING FROM CHAPTER	1	2	3	_____
USEFUL LANGUAGE	1	2	3	_____

ADDITIONAL COMMENTS ABOUT CONTENT

_____

_____

_____

RATING KEY

1 = NEEDS IMPROVEMENT/PRACTICE   2 = GOOD   3 = EXCELLENT